God's Guarantees **Devotional**

Promises of God

A Survival Guide for Walking-the-Walk.

Copyright © 2023 by Geoffrey Kilgore
God's Guarantees Devotional – Promises of God

ISBN 9798850776510
All rights reserved.

No part of this book may be reproduced in any form or by any electronic or mechanical means, including information storage and retrieval systems without written permission from the author, except for the use of brief quotations in a book review.

Dear Reader,

How would you like some amazing guarantees that only God can give. They're life-changing in substance and if you take them for what they are, you will experience a growth in your walk with God.

This is a **150 Day Devotional** on the Promises of God. It goes hand in hand with my book **GOD's GUARANTEES** – Promises of God.

Hope you enjoy it.

Thank you for reading this Devotional.

If you haven't read my book **God's Guarantees**, I would love for you to check it out. This Devotional was based on that book.

You can find **God's Guarantees** by Geoffrey Kilgore on Amazon.

Also, I would also love to hear from you. You can reach out to me via email at:

gkwalkingthewalk@gmail.com

Day 1 → <u>One Small Step At A Time</u>

<u>Proverbs 3:5,6</u> → *Put your whole trust in God with everything that's in you. Don't just rely on your own understanding of each situation. In all your* ways (your plans, your paths, the decisions you make), *acknowledge God* (invite him into the middle of your situation, declaring him Lord over your circumstances). *Do this and <u>he will guide and direct your steps</u>.*

Sometimes, it seems like we just can't see the path ahead of us. There's no direction in God's Word. We can't hear his voice. We're just plain stuck.

But you wanna know something? → God already knows what's up ahead, and sometimes all we'll get from him is one tiny step to take. That's all...just one tiny step.

But, since it's not the grand revelation we were hoping for, we can easily miss it. It's failing to see and take that one tiny step God gives us that can cause us to lose out on a blessing.

There's a reason for that small single step. God in his wisdom knows that's all we can handle. So, put your foot out and just take that one step. Then he'll give you another.

And here's another thing → We can rely too much on our <u>own judgment</u> when we make plans and decisions in our lives. <u>We forget to invite God into the mix</u>. So, who ends up directing our steps? We do. And that can get us into messes.

To make things worse, when things aren't going according to our plan, we sometimes push harder on that door that maybe God is closing. This is where many people miss out on God's blessings – when he closes that door, it's for our own good. He has other blessings in store for us, so it would be foolish to manipulate the circumstances just to force that door back open, right? I mean, either God's in control...or...we are. Which is it for you?

<u>Anything under God's control is never out of control.</u>

Day 2 → <u>Striving and Struggles</u>

<u>Mathew 6:26</u> → *Look at how God takes care of the birds of the air. They don't need to plant, or harvest, or store up food in barns. Yet your father in heaven feeds them. Don't you realize that you are worth far more than a flock of birds? How much more will he take care of you?*

Do you know what God's original intent for humanity was, way back at the beginning? It was to supply all their needs and take really good care of them. God's original plan when he created mankind was for them to live on earth, happy and stress-free, having a beautiful relationship with him.
He provided them with trees and plants to feed them. All they had to do was gather and eat. They didn't even have to sow crops or toil to earn a living. God never intended them to struggle for a living or to barely make it. He simply wanted them to enjoy living in his blessings...to let him provide for them.

That's amazing when you think about it. That's how much God wants to take care of us. The question is – Are we going to let him?

Maybe you've heard the phrase, "Let go and Let God."
There's a lot of truth to that phrase. It requires us to stop our striving to make it in life, to let go of struggling, to put it all in God's hands, and let him take care of us. He knows how and he wants to do it.

But you know what we often do? We take back those things we entrusted into God's hands. Why is that? Could it be we struggle to trust that he knows what's best? Could it be that we just don't trust God to look after our concerns?

Here's the thing → trusting God is a really big deal to him. He knows that at the root of trust is *surrender*. Many of us think we're surrendered to God, but if we don't fully trust him with our lives, how can we be? I think we need to wrestle with this issue until it's settled in our hearts. Do we truly trust God? Are we truly surrendered to him? How about you? Do you trust God? Are your surrendered?

<u>***Faith is trusting God when you don't understand His plan***</u>.

🌳 Day 3 → <u>Want God's Help? Then learn to *'throw'*</u>

<u>**1 Peter 5:7**</u> → *Cast (throw) <u>all</u> of your cares (all of your worries, concerns, anxieties, and fears) onto God. For he cares about you deeply, and watches over you with profound interest in your welfare, because you matter to him.*

What does that verse say we should do? → Throw, literally throw <u>all</u> that stuff that's bothering us off ourselves and onto God. Why? Because he cares enough about us to not let us carry all that stuff by ourselves.

And you know what? That doesn't mean to throw those burdens onto friends, or loved ones (as good at advising they might be). It doesn't mean to throw them onto a therapist (as much as they may help us), and it doesn't mean to give them over to fate or anything else. No...God is specifically saying to throw them onto him...only him.

Besides, if you've given your worries and fears to God, then, guess what...you're no longer carrying them. He is.

So, look at your hands, your shoulders, your back. Are you carrying anything? Hopefully not. You should feel lighter. You're burden-free.

That's the way it should be, don't you agree? That's the way God designed us – to live our lives without stress, worry, or fear. But living in this world is hard enough, right? Sometimes we need someone greater than us to help carry the load. Lucky for us, God's volunteered for the job.

Remember this→ God never intended us to carry our burdens all by ourselves. So, let's check ourselves. Let's make sure we're *<u>throwing</u>* our cares and concerns onto God. He's offering to carry them for us.

<u>Trust is giving our cares to God. Faith is leaving them there</u>.

Day 4 → It's All In The Word 'Let'

Colossians 3:15 → **_Let_** *(allow) the peace that Christ gives <u>rule</u> and reign over your thoughts and emotions.*

Do you see that word _'let'_? It means it's up to us to <u>allow</u> it to happen...to let Jesus' peace have supreme sovereign reign over all our troubled thoughts. It means peace gets to rule our hearts, it gets to have the last say, not worry or fear. But, God won't do it for us. Just as that verse says, it's up to us.

You might be thinking, *"I try but I can't help it. I keep going back to what's troubling me."*

I get it, we all do it, but just know this → God is well aware of your struggles and so He gives you <u>His</u> strength to handle it. Look at this promise below, that he gives us.

Colossians 1:11 → *God will strengthen you <u>with his own power</u>,* (so that you will have <u>his strength</u> within you and his strength becomes your strength). *<u>Then</u>, you won't give up when trouble comes, but instead, you'll have all the patience and endurance you'll need,* (being steadfast and constant).

Do you see the key to that verse? God will give us *<u>his</u>* strength, and his strength becomes our strength.

There's an old saying→ *"Give God <u>your</u> weakness and he'll give you <u>his</u> strength."* It sounds simple...and it is...sort of.
All we have to do is truly believe it and receive it for ourselves.

But, maybe that's really the issue...<u>believing</u>. Believing is a choice we make. So is doubting. Which one are we going to choose? Believing isn't any harder than doubting. And if you think about it, doubting will get you nowhere...believing will get you everywhere.

<u>***Believing isn't based on blind-faith, blind-faith is based on believing.***</u>

🌳 Day 5 → *"How do you enter God's presence???"*

Guess what? You're already there! Through Christ, you belong in the very throne-room of God. You're sitting with him in heaven right now.

Say whaaat??? I get what you're thinking. It's crazy! But I didn't make this up. God said it. Read this verse below:

Ephesians 2:6 → *Because we're united with Christ, God raised us from eternal death <u>together</u> with Christ when he was resurrected, and he <u>seated us together with him</u> in the heavenly realm.*

What's Christ seated on? A throne…in the heavenly realm, in the highest place of honor…at the right hand of God. (See Ephesians 1:20) So, even though it seems impossible, we're seated right next to Jesus, right now in that very place.

How can that be? Well, it's important to see things that pertain to our lives not only from an earthly perspective, but also from a heavenly one.

If God sees you seated with his Son in the spiritual realm of his throne-room in heaven, then we need to believe it from a spiritual perspective.

"Well, I don't know if I can. That's pretty weird!"

Yes, you can. I mean think about it, when an astronomer says that there's a galaxy invisible to the human eye that's 8 billion light years away, do you accept it as true? Yes. How do you accept it? By faith. After all, he's an astronomer, he knows what he's talking about, right? Just do the same with what God's promises, after all, God's the one who made that galaxy and he certainly knows what he's talking about. Shouldn't we believe him more than that astronomer?

If you really think about it, believing is no harder than doubting. The only difference between the two is…a choice.

> ***Faith is not believing that God can. It is knowing that God will.***
> Ben Stein

🌳 Day 6 → <u>The Recipe For Success</u>

<u>Joshua 1:7,8</u> → Be <u>careful</u> to <u>obey</u> <u>all</u> the instructions God gives you in his Book. Don't <u>waver</u> nor <u>deviate</u> from them, not even a small amount. <u>(If) you do these things</u>, THEN you'll have insight and <u>you'll prosper and succeed in everything you do</u>.
Also, <u>study</u> God's Book of Instructions. <u>Ponder and think about it</u> often throughout your days and nights, <u>so that you will be sure to</u> do everything written in it. <u>Only then</u> will you prosper, do well in life, and succeed in all you do.

I know I underlined a bunch of words in that promise, but pay attention to them. They are the keys to the guarantee held within it. **Twice in that passage** God says we'll prosper and succeed and do well in life *if* we:
1) Simply do what God tells us to do, <u>without wavering</u> or straying.
2) Study his Book of Instructions and think about it to understand it, so we'll be <u>sure</u> to do it.

You know what *wavering* is? It's riding the fence between obedience and disobedience. Sometimes we'll do what God says and sometimes we'll do our own thing. There's no consistency. That's wavering.

So, here's the thing: If you want that promise of prosperity and success to become a reality in your life, then you can't *waver* from God's instructions. No wavering or deviating allowed. God says it's an all or nothing deal. He'll do his part, *if* we do ours.

By the way, do you know what the word '<u>**study**</u>' means in that verse?
It means we're not just opening God's Word and randomly picking something to read. Nope, that won't work here. Instead, we have to <u>know</u> and <u>understand</u> what the passages mean and then <u>chew on it over and over</u> in our minds and hearts <u>so that we'll be sure</u> to apply it to our lives.
That's what's going to lead to blessings and increase in our lives. If we would just follow the recipe that God has laid out for us, then we'll prosper and succeed in everything we do. God guarantees it.

Trust and obey...for there's no other way...to be happy in this crazy mixed-up world...so just trust and obey.

🌳 Day 7 → "I don't get it. How do I receive <u>God's strength</u>?"

How do we receive anything into our life? We open our hands, our hearts, our minds and just take it in. Receiving strength from God is *not* because we '*will*' it to happen. No, it's trusting God to give it to us…to give us *his* strength.

You already know this: We can't fight our battles with our <u>own strength</u>. It has to be *his* <u>strength in us</u>, right? Well, how on earth do we do that? Take a look at the verse below:

<u>Zechariah 4:6</u> → *It's not going to happen by your own strength nor by any other power, but <u>it will happen by my Spirit</u>, says the Lord.*

And this verse:
<u>Ephesians 3:16</u> → *God will empower you with powerful miraculous inner strength <u>through his Spirit</u> (living within you).*

That's how we do it…God's strength becomes our strength through his Spirit living within us.

God's strength is a distinct force apart from our own strength. It's a supernatural result of his Spirit residing in us giving us his power, and it's expressed within us through his Spirit.

We should be able to feel it, right? If it's God's strength within us, then shouldn't it feel different from our own strength? After all it's a supernatural strength.

You know what I think? We need to get used to living in his strength. Either we get up each day and live out the day in our own strength or we do it with God's strength mixed in. I know one thing's for sure, I can't do it on my own. How about you?

So, let's look for it, expecting to feel it, expecting it to affect the outcomes in our daily situations. Let's live in his strength.

> ***Be strong in the Lord** (meaning – live in his strength, making his strength your strength), **and be empowered with his power.*** Ephesians 6:10

Day 8 → Corrie Ten Boom once wrote:
"Worry doesn't empty tomorrow of its sorrow. It empties today of its strength."

Did you know that God is adamantly against worry? Jesus, Paul, and the apostles, as well as several Old Testament writers all spoke against it.

I think most of us worry without realizing we're just filling in the gap of not trusting God. We treat it like it's an option, that we're free to worry if we choose to. But nowhere in God's Word does it tell us to worry.

People think they have a lot to worry about in their lives, but you know what Mark Twain once said. "*I have known a great many troubles, but most of them never happened.*" That leaves a whole lot of wasted time worrying, doesn't it?

So, what are we supposed to do?
Look at this guarantee:
Psalm 55:22 → *Give to God* (meaning, release into his hands and let go of) *all your worries and burdens* (those things that weigh you down). *If you do this he will take care of you* (meaning, he'll hold you up, sustain you, so you'll make it through). *In fact, he will never allow his righteous ones to be shaken* (meaning to slip or fall flat on their faces).

According to that promise, this is what God will do for you?
1) He'll take good care of you and sustain you so you can make it through the tough times. It's in his heart to do so.
2) He won't let you fall flat on your face. You're not going to fail…unless *you* let it happen.

What does God expect you to do?
1) Let go of (completely release) your worries and burdens by putting them into God's hands.
2) Make sure you're one of the '*righteous ones*' mentioned in that verse. How? → By continually doing the things he tells you to do. That's what '*righteous*' means (you're consistently doing what is right).

Worried thoughts are notoriously inaccurate. Renee Jain

Day 9 → <u>One Of My Favorite Guarantees:</u>

<u>Psalm 32:8</u> → *I, God, <u>will guide you</u>* (meaning - make plain and show you the way) *along the paths you should choose* (the roads you should travel, the decisions you should make, the course of life you should take). *Along the way, I will <u>instruct you</u>* (meaning - to give you insight into your circumstances) *and I will <u>teach you</u>* (meaning - to point the way out as if by pointing a finger) *and I will advise you as you go. And, my eye will be upon you, <u>to watch over you</u>* (to make sure you're safe and staying on the right path). ***But make sure <u>you don't act like a senseless horse</u>*** *that lacks understanding, that needs a bit in its mouth to keep it under control or else it will not come with you.*

I know, it's a long verse, but <u>don't let it slip by</u>.
Here are the promises God makes to us in that verse.
1) God will <u>show us</u> and make clear to us the paths we should choose
2) God will <u>guide us</u> all along the way so we're not alone, nor directionless.
3) Along the way he promises to <u>give us insight</u> (an accurate perception) of our circumstances.
4) As we go, he promises to <u>point out the way</u> as if using his finger to point, so there's no confusion.
5) Along the way he promises to <u>watch over us</u> to protect us and make sure we stay on the right path.

Want God to lead you? All you have to do is make the *choice* to *let* God do those 5 things in your personal lives. What would keep those things from happening? – not deciding to make the choice.

Think about it, what more could we ask for if we're seeking guidance from anyone? I say hire him as your guide. His rates are low and he's the best in town. ☺

<u>Don't ask God to guide your steps if you're not willing to take a walk.</u>
    Michael Mcafee

🌳 Day 10 → Remember God all along the way

You know what? It's God who causes us to be blessed, to succeed and to prosper in life. So, don't take the credit for it. Stay humble. Give him the honor. The verse below says it all:

Deuteronomy 8:18 → *Don't forget it's the Lord, your God. He is the one that gives you the power and the ability to accumulate wealth and make you successful.*

And how about this verse:
James 1:17 → *Every good thing we have flows down from our Father in heaven…*

This is where having a humble heart is critical as we succeed and prosper in life. Humility is a big thing to God.
I mean, what led to the rebellion in heaven? It was pride. I think that's why God says he hates pride and arrogance so much (See Proverbs 8:13), because it brought so much destruction to heaven and earth.

Plus, God will reward you for being humble. Look at the guarantee below. It's amazing:

Proverbs 22:4 → *The reward for being humble and deeply respecting of God in your life will be wealth, prosperity, honor and an abundantly fresh and flowing life.*

Wow! Did you catch that? Wealth, prosperity, honor and an abundant life. Who doesn't want all that in their life, right?

If that's what you want, then do this:
1.) Be humble. → The Greek meaning of the word *'humble'* is having an honest view of yourself, not thinking you're more important than others. It's giving more honor, and value, and importance to God and other people than you do yourself.
2.) Live with deep *respect* for God. That word *'respect'* in the Hebrew means to use serious caution and self-evaluation to avoid anything that would offend or grieve God.

When you wake up each morning, let your first thought be THANK YOU

🌳 Day 11 → <u>What to do with *trouble* when it comes.</u>

One thing would be to <u>call on God</u>. He's invited us to do so. He says so in the guarantee below:

<u>Psalm 50:15</u> → *<u>Call on me</u> when you're going through distress or trouble. Do this and I will <u>rescue</u> you and you will end up <u>giving me honor</u>*.

Sidenote: The Hebrew word for '*rescue*' in that verse means '*to remove*'. This could mean God removing the trouble from us, or God removing us out of the trouble. Either way, we're rescued, right?

What should we do with that promise? 3 things:
1) <u>Call out</u> to God (not anywhere else but God).
2) <u>Expect</u> him to rescue us because he says he will.
3) <u>Give</u> him the glory when he does.

Another thing would be to make God our <u>refuge,</u> and our <u>strength</u>, and our <u>help.</u> Take a look at the promise below:

<u>Psalm 46:1</u> → *God is our <u>refuge</u>* (meaning - in his presence is safety and rest and peace) *and he is our <u>strength</u>* (his strength becomes our strength - physically, emotionally, and spiritually). *And he is <u>always ready to help us</u> whenever we have trouble*.

When trouble steps into our life, God will do 3 things:
1) He'll be a <u>refuge</u> from the storm.
2) He'll strengthen us so we'll make it through the storm.
3) He'll be right there, <u>ready to help us.</u>

Luckily for us, God volunteered for the job. Now…are you going to take him up on it? If you do, then there should be no reason why you should be alone, weak, or helpless, right?

<u>When you feel your drowning in life's situations, don't worry, your life-guard walks on water.</u>

🌳 Day 12 → <u>Want To Succeed And Prosper</u>?

You know what? God wants us to win at life, so he gave us this passage below to lead us to success, prosperity and blessings.

<u>Psalm 1:1-3</u> → *A person will be blessed <u>if</u> they don't live their life according to the advice of people who rebel against God, nor hang around people who continually choose to do wrong over right.*
<u>Instead</u>, that person finds pleasure in following God's instructions, meditating and thinking about them often through their days and nights.
*That person will be well watered, just like a tree that's planted by a stream of water; it will produce beautiful fruit in its season and its leaves will not wither. In fact, <u>everything that person does will **succeed** and **prosper**</u>.*

Want to prosper and succeed in life? Then, do what's written in that promise:
1) Watch out where you get your advice from, whether it's the tv, or radio, and especially from people that aren't interested in following God.
2) Watch out who you hang out with, especially people that choose to live wrongly before God.
3) Find pleasure in doing God's Word and make an effort to think about it throughout the day.

What will these 3 things do for you?
They'll cause you to be a wise and fruitful person in life (like that tree); **plus**, you'll progress in your endeavors, <u>prospering</u> and <u>succeeding</u> at whatever you do. Who doesn't want that, right?

People can succeed and prosper their own way or God's.way. I know which way I'd choose. How about you?

<u>To be a success in God's eyes is really the ultimate success.</u>

🌳 Day 13 → Are You Confident?

1 John 5:14,15 → *This is the <u>confidence</u> (the certainty) we have when we approach God in prayer. If we ask anything that <u>pleases him</u> and is <u>in agreement with his will</u>, then <u>we can be sure</u> that he has heard us. And, if we know that he's heard us, then <u>we can be sure</u> that he will grant our requests.*

Are you confident when you approach God in prayer that you're going to receive what you ask for?

How would you like to be sure God hears your prayers and answers them?

Then here are the **criteria** in that promise that God says will guarantee he hears us and will grant our request.:

1) Ask for <u>things that would bring God pleasure</u> to give them to us.
2) Ask for <u>things that are in agreement with his will</u>, since he knows what's best for us.
3) Check to see if you have the <u>confidence and certainty that God heard you</u>.

Do these 3 things and according to this promise, you can be certain to get what you ask for from God.

I'm sure you already know this, but let's not treat God like a genie-in-the-bottle. I think sometimes we can throw God our spiritual wishbones.

As we mature in our faith, God's will in our lives becomes our utmost desire. We ask for things we know are in his will. We begin to see God answering our prayers more clearly and frequently because his desires become our desires.

So in our prayers, let's remember to align our requests with his will and then watch what God does. Pretty simple, isn't it?

<u>The value of persistent prayer is not that He will hear us but that we will finally hear him.</u>

Day 14 → What Are You Feeding?

It's been said: *"Feed your faith and starve your doubt."*

I think some of us might look a little gaunt these days because we're feeding our doubt and starving our faith.

Why don't we do the opposite? Let's feed on what God says in his Word...then believe it and confess it in our hearts...continually. That's what it means to feed our faith...and starve our doubts.

Just remember this: To God, trusting him is a really big deal. I mean, it's a REALLY big deal to him. He makes that clear all through the Bible.

The fact is, God is greatly honored when we trust in what he says he'll do for us. But there's more to it than that. God knows that trusting him will help us, by taking our eyes off our problems. Plus, it helps us bring God into the center of every situation. And that's just where he likes to be – in the center of our lives.

Just look at the Israelites when they were in the desert, heading to the Promise Land. They weren't allowed to enter it and enjoy the blessings of that land and the life God wanted to give them. Why? They were focused on their problems, and it fed their doubt and starved their faith.

They dishonored God by <u>not trusting him</u>. He was ready to give them a land of abundance. Had they just trusted in what he said he'd do for them, they would've had a great life...not wandering around in a hot, desolate desert for years on end.

In fact all through the Bible, you can read about amazing things God did for people...all because they trusted him and did what he told them to do. So, you know what we need to do? Trust him. Feed our faith and enter into his abundant life of blessings.

> ***Feed your faith daily and you will no longer hunger after the things of this world.***

🌳 Day 15 → Remember This Promise?

<u>Proverbs 3:5,6</u> → *Put your trust in God with everything that's in you. Don't just rely on your own understanding and judgment of each situation. In all your ways (your plans, your paths, the decisions you make), acknowledge God (invite him into the middle of your situation). Do this and <u>he will guide and direct your steps</u>.and smooth out and level the path you're traveling.*

We're so used to controlling our lives that it's hard to put anything that is a concern to us into God's hands and completely let go of it. Would you agree?
We tend to take it back again and try to make it all work out ourselves, especially if we think God is being too slow.

Then we realize what we're doing and give it back to him once again…for a while, and then we grab it back once more. Over and over we do this…let go, then take it back again.

You know what? God knows what he's doing. He just smiles at us and tries to remind us that he has perfect timing and that he can handle things on his own. He just wants us to believe it, trust it, rest in it.
        God says, *Trust me and I'll show you.*
There's another thing we get hung up on. We tend to want God to fix the problem <u>the way *we* want it fixed</u>. But God's way of doing things isn't our way of doing things and the sooner we accept that fact, the more we'll let go and let God do what he wants, while we get on with the business of watching for his blessings.

That verse above isn't just something to read and store away. No, it has to be up front and present in our lives every day. Do you see that last part of that verse? The Hebrew meaning of God *'directing our steps'* also includes him smoothing out the path we're on. Expect him to do that. It's your God-given right when you apply that verse to your life. It will make the journey so much easier. So claim it. Let him clear out the obstacles and make your path smooth.,l

God has a plan. Trust it. Live it. Enjoy it.

Day 16 → If the evil-one is so powerful, then why would he flee from measly little you?

I'll tell you why. It's because you've surrendered your **'self'** (your self-will) to God's will, so the evil-one has less influence on you now.
It doesn't mean he won't try to tempt you to let *'self'* take over, but because you've surrendered yourself to God, it means you're no longer surrendering to the whims of your *'self'* or the influence of the enemy.
Take a look at these two verses below:

<u>Ephesians 4:27</u> → *Don't give the evil-one the <u>opportunity</u>* (don't make it easy for him) *to defeat you.*

<u>Ephesians 6:11</u> → *Put on (wear) <u>all</u> of God's armor,* **so that** *you can <u>fight</u> against the devil's schemes and tricks.*

Those two underlined words <u>*"so that"*</u> in that second verse are important. It means, you have to do a specific thing <u>*so that*</u> you'll get a specific result.
In other words, if you want to be successful in your fight against the enemy's schemes and tricks, then you'll have to <u>*put on*</u> God's armor. Don't store it in your closet. Wear it.

So, when you put thse two verses together, this is what will help you:
1) Don't give the devil the <u>opportunity</u> to mislead you. Don't even get near the line of temptation, let alone cross it.
2) Wear *all* of God's <u>armor</u> so you can protect yourself. (To know more about God's armor read Ephesians 6, starting at verse 11)

Simple, right? – Wrong!
Because our sin-bent nature can crop its ugly head up. When that happens, we tend to get sidetracked. We tend to be less vigilant, less wary of the enemy. I would say wearing the armor of God daily is a discipline we have to learn. Not giving the enemy the *'opportunity'* to defeat us depends on it. What are you wearing today?

> ***<u>When you put on the full armor of God, you're telling the Devil that he has to go through Jesus to get to you.</u>***

🌳 Day 17 → Here's A *'Don't Let'* Verse

John 14:27 Jesus speaking→ *"I am leaving you with this gift – peace of mind (your thoughts) and peace of heart (your emotions). And my peace that I give you (the peace that comes from me) is not the same as the peace the world offers. So, receive it, and **don't let** your heart be troubled or afraid.*

Did you notice that we don't have to work at getting the peace that Jesus is offering? It's a gift. Unbelievers do all sorts of things to get peace like meditation and mind-body exercises. But the peace Jesus gives is different. He said so. There's no effort involved. None. We just simply receive it. Simple, right?

What we do have to work hard at, however, is not allowing our hearts to return to mulling over what's troubling us. That's the hard part, isn't it?
So, how do we do that? → It's done by making a choice – a choice to *not let* our hearts be troubled, and instead, capture those troubling thoughts and emotions every time they appear. Then, we give them back to God, releasing them into his hands and letting go once again. It's an ongoing process, over and over again, but the more we do it, the easier it becomes.

You probably already knew that, but it's good to hear it again...and again...and again. Why? Because it's hard to do. We often give our worries and fears to God, then take them back again, out of God's hands and back into our own. So, let's make the choice not to let that happen. Ok?
I've always liked the phrase: *'Let go and Let God'.* It's simple and profound. Why? Because when we stop clinging to control over our lives and just *let* God have his way with us, wonderful things start to happen. God can finally work his perfect will in us. We're no longer standing in the way of his supernatural power moving in our lives.

Let's do the *'don't let'*, and let's do it well. Let's not let our hearts be troubled. That will only happen when we *'Let go and Let God.'*

Sometimes we have to let go of what's hurting us, even if it hurts us to let go.

🌳 Day 18 → <u>Want God To Guide Your Steps</u>?

Isaiah 30:21 God speaking → *You'll hear a word behind you telling you, "This is the way you should go. Walk in this direction."*

You know what's interesting about that verse? Notice the words, *"<u>behind you</u>"*. It infers that the person has gone in the wrong direction. They've left God *behind*. They've gotten off God's path and onto their own path. Instead of hearing God in front of them, because he's leading, now they hear him calling after them. Bottom-line is we all need spiritual hearing-aids.

Part of it, I think, is that many of us find it hard to trust anyone else's judgment but our own. We forget to invite God into the middle of our situation. So, who ends up directing our steps? We do. We push our way along, expecting God to bless us, even though he's been left behind in the dust.

This is where many people miss out on God's blessings. It would be foolish to push our way through and manipulate the circumstances. I mean, it really comes down to this – either God's in control...or...we are. Which is it for you?

You know what? God knows what he's doing. He just smiles at us and tries to remind us that he wants to lead us and have us follow, that he has perfect timing, and that he can handle things on his own. We just need to believe it, trust it, rest in it.

If we would just do that, our lives would be so much less complicated, don't you think? Truly if we could get out of God's way, he would have the freedom to work in our lives.

People blame God for the problems in their lives. *'After all,'* they say, *'if God's in control, then he must have allowed this to happen to me.'* The truth is, we often won't allow him to have control. We cling to it ourselves and consequently get ourselves into messes. Don't let that happen to you.

<u>Prayer is speaking to God, meditation is listening to Him.</u>

🌳 Day 19 → Don't Ask God To Guide Your Steps If You're Not Willing To Move Your Feet.

Sometimes we get so tired from trying to figure out what direction to go, we don't feel like taking the steps once God shows us what they are, especially if it involves a bit of effort or challenge on our part. Ever felt that way? Here's a <u>guarantee</u> that will help us:

<u>Isaiah 58:11</u> → *God will <u>continually</u> lead you and guide you as you go, and <u>he will satisfy your needs</u> when you're in that dry parched land, giving you <u>renewed strength</u>. In fact, you'll be just like a well-watered garden, <u>like a spring that never goes dry</u>.*

What's in this promise for you?
1) God promises he'll guide you and lead you <u>continually</u> as you make your way along the path you're on. He'll be your personal guide. Hire him, he's free.
2) When you feel worn out and dried up, he'll give you <u>renewed strength</u>. That means he'll restore the strength you used to have and make it new again.
3) You'll be like a lush garden that has plenty of water, like a spring that continually produces water that refreshes. Instead of parched and dry, you'll be <u>refreshed and well satisfied</u>.

You know what? God originally designed us to live a stress-free life. He didn't create us to have worry and fear wreaking havoc on our minds and bodies, draining us of strength and leaving us parched and dried-up. His original plan was to take good care of us so we could enjoy life, and enjoy his company. Remember he walked and talked with the first two humans.

Let's let God satisfy our needs. Let's claim that promise for ourselves and sit back, rest, and watch with confidence, trusting God to do what he promises in that verse. Trust in God to lead you. We can see a little bit down the road, but God can see around every curve.

<u>God will take you through places you don't understand just to bring you to places he wants you to be</u>.

Day 20 → Be A Little Selfish

You might be thinking, *"Isn't that kind of selfish, to be asking for God to prosper me?"*

The answer is "*No*". Why is that? → Because God tells us over and over again what he wants to do for us. He wants to prosper us, and he expects us to ask for it. He's always made it clear throughout the Bible that he'll pour out blessings on his *obedient* children. What's key here is the "O" word...*obey*. You want to prosper and do well in life? → Do what God says.

And what is *prosperity* anyway? In our culture *prosperity* means to become wealthy and have a lot of things. But the Bible's idea of prospering is to do well in all areas of our lives – in family, work, relationships, and yes, financially.

To prosper God's way, all we have to do is follow what he tells us to do (obey his instructions), believe his promise, and receive his blessings. Pretty simple right?

Just be careful to see your blessings as God sees them. For example, if you were involved in an accident and lost your leg, God may choose to use you through that situation. Can you see it as a blessing from God? It takes spiritual maturity to do that, doesn't it? But, what's the alternative – getting angry at God? If God is trying to turn your lemons into lemonade, then stop seeing your situation as a lemon, and start seeing it as lemonade. After all, how can we receive something that is given to us to bear if we *don't* trust the giver of the gift?

Not to be redundant here, but that's another major key to living this life on earth...faith. Do we truly believe that verse that says *we live our lives by faith, not by sight* (not by how things appear). I think we need to learn to be content along each part of our journey through life. In a way, that's part of prospering.

The question is, if God allows you a lemon, are you going to consider it a gift and allow him to make lemonade out of it?

Day 21 → Are You Ready To *Roll With The Rock*?

Psalm 37:5 → *Commit everything you do to the Lord.* (Hebrew meaning- 'roll' each of your concerns off of you and onto God). *Trust him with it all. Do that and he will help you* (Hebrew meaning- He will work it all out for you. He will attend to it and put it all in order.)

Wanna know the most amazing thing about God?
He's able to turn any situation around for our good. Any situation! And he loves to do it. All he's waiting for is for us to give him the chance. We need to *roll* all those concerns that have been weighing us down, onto God. Can you picture yourself doing that?

Then we need to trust him with them, leaving them in his hands. Are you doing that? If you are, then God says he'll help to work it all out for you. He'll attend to it. He'll put it all in order. That's what the Hebrew meaning of that phrase *"he will help you"* actually means. Wow! That takes the load off our shoulders, doesn't it?

Sometimes we blow it in life and as a result, we've made a mess of things. That's the chance God's been waiting for.

God always keeps his promises of helping us get back on the right track. He wants to bring us right back into his sphere of blessings where he can care for us and protect us.

But, you know what keeps God's blessings and protection away? If he tells us to go one way (to keep us out of trouble) and we continue to go the opposite, things aren't going to go so well for us.

So, don't be messin' with the blessin'. Get back on the right path that leads you right back into his plan of blessings for your life and let him turn those lemons into lemonade. How do you do that? It all starts with making a U-turn. That's called *repentance* – getting back on his path, and then committing all those burdens we've been carrying to God, and rolling them onto his shoulders so he can carry them.

Let's face it, being under God's care and protection, and letting him work out the details of our lives is the safest place to be in this crazy mix-up world. I wouldn't want to be anywhere else. How about you?

Day 22 → Whatcha Worried About?

Matthew 6:34 Jesus seaking→ *So, don't worry about what's going to happen tomorrow or the days thereafter. Each day brings enough troubles of their own.*

When you think about it, worrying is moving into tomorrow ahead of time. It's carrying tomorrow's load with today's strength, and that's carrying two days at once.

I like what Dale Carnegie said: *"Today is the tomorrow you worried about yesterday."* Isn't that the truth!!!

Notice that Jesus says in that verse that each day will bring its own set of troubles. It's just a fact of life, isn't it. The question is, does that mean we need to worry about them? Nope, because God has specific things he tells us to do with all the troubles that come our way...and worry isn't one of them.

1 Peter 5:7 → *Cast (throw) all your worries and concerns onto God* (meaning - release them into God's hands and let him have all your worries, anxieties and concerns). *Because he cares about you with deep affection* (and is aware of everything that concerns you).

Psalm 55:22 → *Give to God* (release out of your hands and put into God's hands) *all your worries and burdens* (those things that weigh you down). *Do this and he will take care of you and hold you together.*

3 verses with 2 promises: Do you want to free from worry?
Here's what to do:
1) Throw or roll all those worries and concerns that consume your life onto God...and only him.
2) Entrust them to him *(let go...and let God).*
3) He'll take good care of you and work it all out.

Here's what God promises to do:
1) He'll care enough about you personally to be fully aware of what's going on in your circumstances.
2) He will take good care of you and hold you close through it all.
 The question is...will you believe it?

Pray and Let God Worry. Martin Luther

🌳 Day 23 → <u>Are You Living</u>?

I've always liked this phrase → *"May you live all the days of your life." (Jonathan Swift)*

You know what I find sad about that statement? Many of us don't do it. We miss out on the blessings that God intended for us because we're often too busy to hear his voice. We're so caught up in the events in our lives that we fail to see the important things God wants us to focus on that will lead to the fullness of life.

I think we've become God's family of 'maintenance people'. We're so busy maintaining our homes, our jobs, our hobbies, our kids' sports, our lawns, our workouts, our hair and nails, we barely have time for God.

Yeah, we might get up and open the Bible for 15 minutes and randomly open to a passage. Then after we've read it, we close the book and say a quick prayer, and forget about what we've read. Then it's off to breakfast, or work, or getting the kids to school. We might turn on Christian radio and say a prayer while driving and call it worship.

I think we've lost the awestruck reverence and fear of our almighty God. We fit him in when we have an empty moment in our schedule. But this is God we're talking about, the one who is so holy the angels bow in utter reverence. This is the one who with his words created the expanse of the universe and the DNA strands of the human cell. This is the God, that when he spoke from the mountain, dark swirling clouds, and bolts of lightning along with frightening booms of thunder made the Israelites cower in fear.

"May you live all the days of your life."

If we're going to live the days of our lives, there has to be more to it than this. I mean, where's the power and the victory and the supernatural outcomes that make the Christian life so exciting? Where's the laying down of our lives, the surrender, the sacrifice of 'self'? What!!! Oh…ok…sorry…I'll calm down. Let me catch my breath…Ok…I'm calm now. We can all go on about our day. 😊

Day 24 → God To The Rescue

Take a look at this promise:
2 Timothy 4:18 → *God will rescue me from every evil attack. In fact, he will bring me safely into his heavenly kingdom. So, all glory be to him.*

This is a great promise to declare to ourselves, to God, and to our unseen enemies in the spiritual realm, whenever we're being attacked, just like the apostle Paul is doing in that verse. It strengthens our faith when we do it. Try it. It will feed your faith and starve your doubt. And try it with this next guarantee.

Psalm 138:7 → *Even when my life is surrounded by troubles, you stretch your hand out against my enemies and the power of your right hand saves me.*

The 'right hand' of God, refers to God's strength and power as well as his hand of victory. When kings in the Old Testament were in the midst of a battle, if victory was imminent, they would hold up their hand for their soldiers to see. So it is with us. When God stretches out his hand against our enemies, we can be certain we'll have the victory. We win.

But what if you claim this promise for yourself and the trouble still remains? What then? → You stand strong and wait. That's what you do. You may be surrounded by trouble on all sides and weary from the beating you're taking but be assured, God is never late. He's always on time. He will come to the rescue.

There's always a purpose behind his timing. It might be to test whether you really are trusting him, or maybe it's to teach you something and the trouble you're experiencing is forcing you to pay attention. Whatever the reason may be, you can be certain that God knows what he's doing and it's always to bless you in the end. The question is: Do you believe it?

Sometimes God reaches down to rescue us even when we didn't know we needed rescuing.

🌳 Day 25 → *"Show Me The Money!"*

Do you remember that line from Jerry Mcguire?
There's nothing wrong with having money and good things in your life...as long as they don't have you.
Seeking God <u>first</u> and his right way of living is your <u>safeguard</u> from that happening.

God in his wisdom knew that if he told us to seek him first, it would keep us aimed in the right direction, it would keep us from seeking the riches of this world more than God.

But you know what? Prosperity isn't something we seek after, it's something that comes naturally as a result of following God's way of living. God makes that plain over and over again.

I think sometimes people think, *"If I'm good enough, then God will prosper me."* Well, we don't earn God's blessings of prosperity as a *reward* for doing good things. God doesn't measure our performance and then dole out blessings *only* if we're good. He's just naturally good to us and as a good father, he wants to prosper us and bless us when we follow his directives and stay in obedience to him.

The truth is, God is wise, and his Word holds his wisdom in it. If we put into practice the things he tells us to do in his Word, it will naturally lead us to wise management of our lives as well as the blessings and increase he intended for us.
Read the verse below as <u>God's guarantee to you personally</u>:

<mark>James 1:25</mark> → *Those who look deeply and carefully into God's Word and don't forget what it says, but instead are <u>careful to do it</u>, they will <u>prosper</u> and be <u>blessed</u> in <u>all</u> they do.*

The bottom-line is this: Read (or hear) his Word and do it in your life. Then you'll naturally do well and be blessed. That's God's way of prospering.

You're blessed...so be a blessing.

Day 26 → <u>God Is Mean!!!</u>

Would you agree that God's not vindictive...that he doesn't want to make us pay when we do wrong or offend him? That's just not the heart of God, is it?
But, like a good father, he will use discipline to teach us how to live so we can stay in his sphere of blessings.

I think we all need to remember, <u>everything</u> that God tells us to do is for our own good. He's not trying to keep us under his thumb, or squeeze the joy of living out of us, or make life hard for us. He wants us to do what he says because he truly wants us to have an abundant life, to bless us with good things. He doesn't want any '<u>*roadblocks*</u>' to get in the way. He wants his children to do really well in life.

And I'm sure you would agree that when we ignore God and just do what we want without regard to what he wants for us, then we've just put a '<u>*roadblock*</u>' in the path of his blessings?

In fact, if we're not paying attention, those roadblocks may look to us like God just doesn't seem to care about us. He does. It's usually not his fault...it's usually ours. He didn't leave our side...we just got side-tracked and left his side. We created the *roadblocks*, not God.

Some of us might be thinking, *"It's just too hard to live the way God wants me to."*

I get it...sometimes the paths to his blessings aren't easy. But I want you to know if you make the effort to avoid the roadblocks, it will <u>always</u> take you to good places. That's God's heart for you...nothing but good. I'll say it again and again: God is *always* good to us...*all* of the time.

I'm sure none of this is applicable to you at this time in your life, but there can be a time when all of us stray enough from God's paths to create *blessing-blockers* for ourselves. When that happens, the good news is, God allows U-turns, so we can get right back under his wings of protection, and blessings.

<u>***When God seems far away...guess who has moved?***</u>

Day 27 → Scattered Enemies

Deuteronomy 28:1,2 → *God will cause your enemies to be defeated before you. They will attack you from one direction, but they will scatter and flee from you in seven directions.*

Why are your enemies scattering?
Because God is defeating them. They're running from God and they don't even know it. The number *seven* in the Bible commonly signifies 'completeness'. *Scattering* in seven directions means complete and utter defeat of the enemy. That's what we should expect, right?

What a great promise to hold onto. Isn't that what we all want…for our enemies to flee and leave us alone?
However, this verse hinges on a **contingency**. → In the first and second verses of that chapter it says this: → '*If you have an obedient heart and are careful to follow all of God's instructios,.then these blessings will be yours.*' So, don't forget to do that. I'm sure you would agree that if we're not faithful to follow God's instructions, then we probably aren't going to see God scattering our enemies the way we hoped he would. But that's not you or me, because we're one of his faithful ones, right? So, look at this next verse. It applies to us:

Romans 8:31 → *How should we respond and what shall we say about all these wonderful things? If God is for us, then who can stand against us?*

The promise in that verse above is that God is on our side. He wants us to win. And, *if* he's on our side, our enemies don't stand a chance. God always wins the battle…every time.

But we have to be on God's side too. That can only happen when we're staying close to him. **James 4:8** says, '*Stay close to God. If you do, then he will stay close to you.*' You know what? That will happen for us personally when we do just what that verse says. So, speak that verse out to yourself. Declare it to your enemies. Feed your faith and starve your doubts.. *"God's on my side. He's fighting the battle for me. No enemy can stand against me."*

The enemy always fights the hardest when we draw closer to God.

🌳 Day 28 → Making God Our Refuge

Psalm 73:28 → *As for me, being in God's presence is all I need. I have made God my refuge and put my full trust in him.*

So, if I were to ask you how to do we make God our refuge, what would you say? I know...it's hard to verbalize, isn't it?

One answer would be to get in God's presence...not in distractions like TV, YouTube, Instagram, Facebook, Golf, etc. (Whoops. Did I say golf? Sorry, I'm not a golfer, so it's easy for me to say that. Ok...take golf off the list.)

Just get in his presence, because if we're smack dab in the middle of his presence, we're safe and we can just rest, even while we're going through the trouble, right?

Ever seen an animal refuge or a bird sanctuary? It's a place where they feel safe, where they can rest and be at peace...no enemy stalking them. That's the way it is when we make God our refuge.

Plus, the Bible also says that in his presence is the fullness of joy. (See Psalm 16:11) It doesn't say we *might* have joy in his presence. No, it says that if we hang out in God's presence, we're *guaranteed* joy. And it's not just a little bit of joy. No, it will fill us to the brim. That's what that word '*fullness*' means in the Hebrew.

And you know what? When we're in God's presence and joy is filling us to the brim, there's absolutely no room left for sadness, despair, hopelessness, or depression. Am I right about that?

So, here's what you and I need to do each and every day:
    1) Make God our refuge.
    2) Stay in his presence.

That's where we'll find peace, safety, rest, and joy.
It's the safest place to be in this crazy mixed-up world we live in.

Sometimes God sends the storms to show us He's the only shelter.

Day 29 → What Does God Expect Us To Do With Worry?

Philipians 4: 6&7 → *Don't let* yourself be worried, or troubled, or afraid about one single thing. Instead, pray about it, telling God what you need. Then, (with faith), thank him for what he's done and is going to do. If you do this, *God's own peace*, which is way beyond our understanding, will guard your thoughts from worry and your hearts from being troubled or afraid; all of this as you live your life united with Christ Jesus.

Remember this: God never condones worry. Nowhere in his Word does he ever tell us to worry. What you just read in that verse is what he expects us to do with our worry and troubled thoughts?
1) Take them to him in prayer. (Giving God all our worries...letting go and letting God have them; letting him keep them...no backsies)

2) Thank him with faith for what he's going to do.

What does God say he will do for us if we do that?
1) He'll give us *his* peace which is different from any other peace we've known. I would venture to say his peace is supernatural.
2) His peace will keep our thoughts from worry and our emotions from being distraught. That's what he wants for us.

There are numerous medical studies that tell of the detrimental effects of worry on our bodies. It can weaken our body's immune systems and wreaks havoc on our heart, our brain, and various other organs.

In fact, God didn't design us to live stressful, worried lives at all. It wasn't part of his original plan. He designed us to be at peace, to be filled with joy at all times. It's hard to imagine, but that was his original plan...before sin entered the picture.

Plus, worry defeats our faith. How can we be worried and be full of faith? The two don't mix...at all. Wouldn't you agree we need to stop talking about how big our problems are and start talking about how big our God is? He deserves it. He's worthy of our good words.

Stop worrying about what can go wrong and get excited about what can go right.

🌳 Day 30 → Do You Know Your ABC's?

If the promises of God are to really sink into our daily lives, maybe we need to practice our **ABC's**

A- Agree with God on what he promises to do.
B- Believe in our hearts that it will happen in our lives.
C- Confess it continually (to feed our faith and starve our doubts).

Here's an example of a promise we can **ABC**:

Would you like to live in complete and total peace all of the time?

Isaiah 26:3 → *God will continually keep in complete and total peace all those who **let** their trust be solely in him* (meaning - who totally rely on him and are completely confident in his wisdom and his ways, his abilities and his power, thus no worries or fear).
*And he will keep in peace all those who **let** their thoughts be fixed on him* (instead of their worries or their fears).

There are two things to see here.
1) What God says he will do for us.
2) What God says we should do for him.

God will do the *keeping-us-in-peace* part
(***if***) we do the *trusting-and-fixing-our-thoughts-on-him* part.

It's kind of amazing how simple it is...yet it can seem really hard at times. What makes it hard is that little tiny word - *"let"*.

We have to *"let"* ourselves completely trust God and totally *"let"* our worries go. We have to *"let"* ourselves fix our thoughts on him and *not "let"* our troubles overwhelm us.

For many of us that can be hard to do. The thing is, though, if we don't allow the *"let"* to happen, then we lose out on a lot of peace that could be flowing through our lives.

Such a simple word – "Let", yet it holds so much potential for allowing us to live a powerful Christian life. That's why I like this phrase so much → ***Let go...and...Let God***

Enjoy the life Jesus died for you to have.

🌳 Day 31 → God Doesn't Hold Back.

Romans 8:32 → *God gave us his greatest treasure as a gift. He did not even spare his own Son but gave him as a sacrifice for us all. Since God did this for us, <u>he certainly won't **hold back** from any other good thing he has to give us</u>.*

Do you think that this pertains *only* to spiritual things? Nope. God's goal in sending Jesus was to get rid of sin and death and restore us back to his original plan he had for humanity. And a large part of that original plan in Genesis was to bless us with good things and take good care of us here on this earth.

Let me ask you this question → What do you think God's plans are for you personally? – Prosperity or Poverty? Take a look at this <u>guarantee</u>:

Jeremiah 29:11 God speaking→ *I know the plans I have for you. I have <u>plans to prosper you</u>, not to cause you calamity or harm; but to <u>give you</u> a future filled with <u>hope</u> and <u>good things</u>.*

We all kind of know that God has plans for us, and that he's never late with his timing.. But we can certainly slow him down and mess up his plans for us by carrying out our own agenda. Have you ever done that...gotten in the way of God's good plans for you? I think we all have. When we do that, it can become a *blessing-blocker*, because now God is not free to carry out his plans. Our plans have superceded his.

People think, *"Well God's in control anyway. He always gets his way in the end."* Maybe, and maybe not. God is not pushy. He speaks with a still small voice and gently nudges us to go his way. It's usually us who are the brash ones, aggressively pushing our own agenda that meet our own needs and desires.

Lucky for us, God allows U-turns, right? We can renew our thinking to align with God's, just as it says in Romans 12:2. If we do that then our plans will naturally align with God's plans for us and that will lead us straight into his sphere of blessings and good things.

<u>God always gives his best to those who leave the choice with him.</u>

Day 32 → I Ain't Got The Spirit

Romans 8:11 → *The Spirit of the living God, who gave life to Christ by raising him from the dead, <u>now lives within you</u>.*

Some of us might be thinking, "*I just don't feel God's Spirit in me. Not at all! Is something wrong with me?*"

Well, we know God doesn't lie. If he says his Spirit lives in us, then he is. Jesus said to a man who brought his son to be healed: "*Anything is possible if a person will just believe.*" You know what the father's response was? "*I do believe but help me overcome my <u>un</u>belief.*"

I love his honesty. Sometimes I think we need to be honest with God, just like that father was. Don't be afraid to tell God the same thing. Notice the man <u>asked</u> Jesus for <u>help</u> with his <u>un</u>belief. Do you think Jesus told him, "*No*"? God is more than happy to do the same for us…to help our unbelief.

If you're struggling with doubt, just tell him. He already knows the thoughts of your heart anyway. He won't frown on you or make you feel guilty. He totally understands you.

Just remember: God wants nothing but good for you all of the time. So, tell him what you think. He'll be glad to help you with any <u>un</u>belief. He won't hold it against you.

Then just wait. Wait for him to act. Look for it. He'll help you to believe. He might just put you in a difficult situation to make that happen, but if we stay calm and cooperate with God, we'll see our faith blossom. Don't be afraid of the hard stuff.

Sometimes I think we try to put on a façade of a happy successful Christian, when inside we're hurting, sad, feeling guilty, or rebellious. Yet because he made us, God already knows what's going on inside our hearts. So, why not be honest with God, ourselves, and others around us?

<u>Faith does not make things easy, it makes them possible.</u>

🌳 Day 33 → Don't Allow Yourself

<u>Exodus 14:13,14</u> → *<u>Don't allow yourself</u> to be afraid in any way. <u>Keep standing strong</u>, firm and <u>confident</u>, and <u>watch</u> God come to your rescue today. <u>God will do the fighting for you</u>. All you have to do is <u>remain calm</u>.*

I know I underligned a lot of words in that verse, but this is a universal promise mentioned over and over again throughout the Bible and each of those words are important:
1) Don't let yourself freak out with fear. <u>Stay calm</u>.
2) Be <u>strong</u> and <u>confident</u> in God.
3) <u>Watch</u> God come to the rescue and do the fighting for you.

Yes, in this passage it was Moses talking to the Israelites who were being chased by a powerful enemy, the Egyptians, and now they're standing at the edge of the Red Sea with nowhere else to escape to. They were cornered. That's exactly how God likes it – when we're cornered and there's nowhere else to turn. When we're weak, he is strong.

You know what the Israelites were doing when Moses said that statement? They were complaining - *"Why did God let this happen to us?"* How about us? Are we complaining about our situation, or are we doing those 3 things listed in that passage at the top of the page.

Don't miss this: Wanna know one of the ways God fights for us? – with his Word. It's truth and the enemy hates truth. If you're getting pounded by the enemy just do what Jesus did when the evil-one attacked him → Go on the <u>offensive</u>.
1) Jesus quoted scripture as a weapon. How was it a weapon? It was truth. The devil hates truth and flees from it because Jesus said there is no truth found in him. None! So, just do the same. Use God's Word as a weapon.
2) Jesus also put his circumstances into the hands of God, trusting him to fight the battle.

So, move into '*offensive mode'*. Do your part – fight back with God's Word. Then, let God do his part – fighting the battle with you and for you.

<u>Remember God's Word is a Sword. Keep it by your side.</u>

Day 34 → God's Love, Kindness, and Goodness

<u>Psalm 32:10</u> → *Those who truly <u>TRUST</u> God* (meaning - who fully rely on him, totally confident in his wisdom, his ways, his abilities and power...thus having no worries or fears), *to them **his love*** (meaning - his guiding, providing, protecting love) *and **his kindness*** (meaning - his goodwill and good intentions) *<u>and</u> **his goodness*** (meaning - his supernatural favor and the giving of good things that will help them thrive, not just survive, but thrive and prosper and do well in life); *these things will <u>surround</u> and <u>fill</u> their lives...all <u>because</u> they trust him.*

If you truly <u>trust</u> him the way that verse says, God promises that he'll do **3 things for you:**

1) His '*love*' will surround your life.
What would that look like for you? Just think about it for a moment. That word '*love*' in the Old Testament is "<u>chesed</u>" and it describes a love the way a father would love his children. He lovingly provides for them, and gives them loving guidance, and he lovingly protects them. If you're trusting God, then expect this for yourself.

2.) His '*kindness*' will surround your life.
This is <u>above and beyond</u> the usual kindness God shows everybody. This is aimed directly at you in such a concrete way that you won't be able to miss it.
This is also part of that Hebrew word "chesed". It includes '<u>goodwill and good intentions</u>' and that's what God will have toward you – nothing but kindness and the best intentions...***if*** you truly trust him. Again, expect this to be part of your daily life.

3) His '*goodness*' (giving of good things) will surround your life.
Many Bible scholars include the word "*goodness*" to describe the Hebrew word "chesed". In the original Hebrew language, it means God giving us <u>good things</u> that will help us <u>thrive</u>, not just survive, but thrive and <u>prosper</u> and <u>do well</u> in life.
So, if you're truly trusting him, then you too can expect good things to show up in your life, every day, to help you thrive and prosper and do well in life. Look for it to happen.

<u>Your loving-kindness is better than life.</u> (Psalm 63:3)– Do we believe it?

Day 35 → God's Strength – Our strength

<u>Colossians 1:11</u> says → <u>*God will*</u> *make you stronger with <u>his</u> strength* (so that his strength is in you, and his strength becomes your strength). *Then, you'll have all the <u>patience</u> and <u>endurance</u> you'll need to make it through.*

How do we get his strength? First, we let go of trying to rely on our own strength and then we ask for his supernatural strength. It takes believing that God will give it. Then we wait for it and expect it.
Remember: It's God who is providing the strength. We don't have to go looking for it. He pours his strength into us. His strength becomes our strength.

What kind of strength is God providing?
Physical strength? Emotional strength? Spiritual strength?

And think about this: God's strength is supernatural. So, it will become supernatural in our own lives as his strength operates in us. You'll know it because of the *"Huh…that's definitely not me. It's gotta be God."* kind-of-thoughts start happening.

And here's another thing: If you're like me, when you're going through troubles, you'll need all the <u>patience</u> and <u>endurance</u> you can get. It'll either come from ourselves or God. Which do you think would be the better source? How many times have I relied on myself during tough times, when I could have been relying on God. Never again. How about you?

By the way, if someone asked you the difference between *patience* and *endurance*, would you know it?
<u>Patience</u> means to put up with and tolerate someone or a situation **without getting upset**.
<u>Endurance</u> means to put up with and tolerate adversity and trouble **without giving up**.

<u>When you are weak, your God is strong. Don't tell God how big your storm is, tell the storm how big your God is.</u>

🌳 Day 36 → The Great Physician's Prescription

Can a proverb be a promise?
Yup, I think so. Because the book of Proverbs holds the wisdom of God, and God's wisdom is truth, and truth means it will always come true. **That's what makes a proverb a promise**…it will always come true.

So, now, read this promise from the book of Proverbs:

Proverbs 17:22 → *A heart that has joy, brings health and healing to the body and soul.*

And take a look at this proverb:

Proverbs 3:24 → *When you sleep you won't be afraid. You'll sleep well because of peace in your heart.*

Medical science has numerous studies on the health benefits of joy and peace. God already knew that. After all, he's our Great Physician, right?

You know what brings about the joy and peace that result in a healthy body and a good night's rest? It's seeking and holding onto God's wisdom, and his wisdom is found in his Word.
After all, God made us and he knows what's best for us. He knows what's going to lead us down the path of his wonderful blessings of health and wellbeing.

If we seek after his prescription of health and take a dose of joy and peace, then we too will have a healthier body and get a good night's sleep. It's a supernatural phenomenon that God put into place, and he expects us to take a good healthy dose of it.

Hey, if our Great Physician is prescribing it, then may he could give us a double dose!

True wisdom begins and ends with God. He will be our peace.

🌳 Day 37 → '*You mean I Can Ask For Anything?*'

Matthew 21:22 Jesus speaking→ *You may ask for <u>anything</u> in prayer, and **if** you believe and have faith, you will receive it.*

Obviously, this is not a 'genie in the bottle' promise, yet I sometimes think we treat it that way, as if God only exists to fulfill our every request. For some reason, people think God should automatically listen to their prayers. After all, he does say, *"You may ask for anything"*, right? But allow me to suggest that we take the time to look up every verse on prayer. I believe we'll be quite surprised at the number of contingencies God puts forth in order for our prayers to be heard and answered.

For example, here's one of those contingencies:

James 4:3 says → *When you ask for things from God, you end up not receiving them because your motives are wrong. You ask for things only to fulfill your own desires, for your own pleasure.*

Some of us might be thinking, *"Wait a second, don't those two verses contradict each other? I mean, first Jesus tells us to ask for things to make us happy. And now the apostle James is telling us not to do that because we're being selfish. What's the deal?"*

(Maybe you don't talk that way, but that's the way I'm writing it.) ☺

It all comes down to <u>motives</u> behind the asking, wouldn't you agree? There's nothing wrong with asking for stuff that will bring us joy, but if it's just a spiritual wishbone to fulfill our own self-centered pleasure rather than fulfill the overall will and pleasure of God in giving it to us, then we may not receive an answer.

Example: If we ask for a Mercedes convertible, rather than a car to get us to work, then we may not get what we want. You get the idea.

So hey, let's not stop asking…let's just ask for the right stuff.

<u>True prayer is asking God for what he wants.</u>

Day 38 → Here's A Way To Build Up Your Faith:

Find a promise of God that speaks to your heart and fills your need. Then, meditate on it and speak it out until it starts to take root and fills your heart. Pretty soon you'll be speaking it from the abundance of your heart. You'll be speaking it in faith.

Then when those arrows of the enemy start flying, you hold that shield of faith up and speak God's Word that flows from your heart.

That's what Jesus did. He used what God calls the Sword of the Spirit which, according to the Bible, is the Word of God (See Ephesians 6:17). It's the offensive weapon that you stab and slice the enemy with.

When Jesus was attacked by the enemy, he replied, *"It is written."* Then he would quote God's Word. The enemy couldn't take the truth because he's a liar. In fact, with one struggle after another, Jesus didn't give in, he just kept slicing and jabbing with that Sword…*"It is written…"* until finally the enemy gave up and left. That's what will happen for us. The light of the truth eliminates darkness wherever it shines.

Here's the thing, though: Jesus quoted scripture to fight the enemy, but it wasn't God's Word alone that made the Sword so effective, it was his faith in God's Word. Just quoting God's Word didn't frighten the enemy. After all he quoted back scripture to Jesus (although it was quoted wrongly). What made him flee was the realization that Jesus had complete faith in what he was quoting. Not only did Jesus know the Word, but he fully believed it. The enemy knew he had lost, because the truth always destroys lies.

So it will be for us. When we put our faith in God's Word and speak it out with full assurance to the evil-one. He might snarl at us, but he'll flee, because truth backed by faith is a potent weapon from a spiritual stand-point. Don't forget that fact. As our daughter's little girl says…***"rememberize"*** it.

<u>Faith is acting like God is telling the truth</u>. Tony Evans

🌳 Day 39 → Wadda Ya Worried About?

Look at what Jesus said

Matthew 6:32 → *Don't allow yourselves to be worried about things, saying, "How are we going to make it?" These worries dominate the thoughts of unbelievers. But your father in heaven already knows all of your needs.*

You know what Jesus is saying here? → Unbelievers worry, but believers don't. Why would they if God *already* knows their needs? We need to ask ourselves why we're worried. Could it be that we just don't trust that God notices us or that he will come through to help us? If you think about it, the only thing that really stands between worry and no-worries…is doubt. Where do you stand?

Jesus said, in Matthew 6:34 → *So, just don't worry about what's going to happen tomorrow or the days thereafter. Each day has enough trouble of its own.*

Notice that Jesus says in that verse that each day will bring its own set of troubles. It's a fact of life. The question is…does that mean we need to worry about them? Nope, because God has specific things he tells us to do with all the troubles that come our way…and *worry* isn't one of them, right?

I wrote this earlier but I think it's worth repeating. → Worrying is moving into tomorrow ahead of time. It's carrying tomorrows load with today's strength – and that's carrying two days at once. That can be exhausting. God never intended for us to do that. As I've said before, God original design for mankind was for us to be stress-free, worry-free, feeling safe and well taken care of by our Father in Heaven. Worry doesn't fit into that picture, does it?

I like what Dale Carnegie once wrote:
"Today is the tomorrow you worried about yesterday."

Day 40 → Give Me Some Power

Ephesians 3:16 → *God will empower you with powerful miraculous inner strength through his Spirit (living within you).*

Some of us might be thinking, *"I don't get it. How does God actually strengthen me?"*

It happens the same way we receive God into our life...by faith. When God adopts us as his children, he promises to live in us by way of his Spirit. We become spiritually alive, no longer dead inside, and now his strength can flow within us...through his Spirit residing in us. But, in order for that promise to come true for you, you'll have to decide whether you believe it...or not. Do you really believe God will empower you with mighty, miraculous, supernatural inner strength through his Spirit within you? If yes, then expect it. There should be some evidence of it, right?

Side-Note: That word '*empower*' in that verse above is the Greek word 'dynamis' which is where we get the word 'dynamite'. It means to infuse with '*mighty, miraculous, forceful power*'. In other words, the inner-strength we're talking about is not 'just enough' strength to barely make it through. Nope, it's mighty and miraculous strength infused with power.

So, it's not just, *"God give me strength."* No, it's *"God you promised that your Spirit living in me will give me mighty and powerful inner strength. So, here I am, God. Give it to me! I want to feel it. I want to see the difference. I'll wait...because I'm expecting you to come through."*

I don't know about you, but I can't live the life God wants me to in this crazy mixed-up world unless I have his miraculous power within me. There are many days when that power just isn't operating in me...at all. Just ask my wife. ☺ And it's not a very good testimony, that's for sure.

The bottom-line as far as I can see is we need God to strengthen us and that will only happen when we believe him for it. And that, in turn, will only happen when we exercise our faith.

Where our strength runs out, God's strength begins.

Day 41 → Here's How To Deal With Our 'Flesh'

Ready for it? Look at this verse:

<u>Jeremiah 17:10</u> → *Search me, God, and know my hidden thoughts. Examine me and know the motives of my heart. And point out anything that may grieve or bother you. Then help me to go down the right path that leads toward your everlasting life.*

WARNING: If you pray something like this and really mean it...you are asking for it (literally and metaphorically speaking...lol). When I started praying this verse, whew, it was humiliating...and... painful. God showed me stuff that I thought I had a handle on. He put people and circumstances in my life just to bring out my fleshly thoughts and behavior. He'll do the same for you...so heed my warning.

It's not a bad thing, though. It's a good thing. It's what the Bible calls the '*sanctification process*' - It's God pointing out the ugly stuff within us, and then *letting* him deal with it so he can make us more like his Son. But it's hard...dealing with all the ugly parts in us. It's not fun. It can become embarrassing, especially when we think we have our spiritual act together.

So, guess what? → We have a <u>choice</u> to make. We can *let* God point all the ugly stuff out to us and then let Him deal with it in us...or not. But just remember, if we don't cooperate with God and let it happen, then all that fleshly behavior just hangs around and gets in the way of us growing up in God and enjoying <u>his</u> <u>peace</u>.

I can give you a guarantee, though. → If you pray that verse out and really mean it from your heart...then God will answer it. If you're really listening and watching for it, he'll point out the fleshly parts of your life for you to see. And if you surrender them to God and let him deal with them in your life, those 'roadblocks' of the flesh will be removed, and the <u>peace</u> will start flowing.

<u>The flesh has to die so that the spirit can live. Kill your flesh or your flesh will kill you.</u>

🌳 Day 42 → Give Me Some Peace

How would you like to have God's peace (not the world's peace) in every situation of your life? Then look at the guarantee below:

2 Thessalonians 3:16 → *May God, who is the author of peace, himself give you his peace at all times and in every situation.*

- Who is giving the peace? - God
- Who's peace are we getting? - God's
- What do we have to do to get it? - Nothing. → Just receive it by faith...believing God will give it to you.
Note: This verse actually starts off like a prayer. The thing is, the apostle Paul, who wrote it, would not have made this statement if he didn't believe God would do it for us. So, we need to believe it and receive it as well.

And you know what? "*At all times*" means exactly what it sounds like...at all times. And, "*In every situation*" means...in every situation. You get the point. So, it might be useful to us to check and see *if* we truly are at peace in the situations we're in. If we're missing that peace, then we need to get it back.

Some of us might be thinking, *"Are you kidding me? How am I supposed to feel peace when I've been really hurt by someone...or...when I'm going through a horrendous trial?"*

Good point. It really is all about having Jesus with us in the boat during the storm, don't you think? Could it be that simple? From my experience and from the experience of others, yes, I think so.
We've already mentioned this verse, but here it is again:

Isaiah 26:3 → *God will continually keep in complete and total peace all those who let their trust be solely in him* (meaning - who totally rely on him and are completely confident in his wisdom and his ways, his abilities and his power, thus no worries or fear). *And he will keep in peace all those who let their thoughts be fixed on him* (instead of their worries or their fears).

That's what we need to do if we want complete continual peace –
Trust Him.

The peace that God gives is so deep, not even the devil can disturb it.

🌳 Day 43 → Time To Get Real

1 Corinthians 6:19 → *Do you not know that you are the temple of the Holy Spirit, whom God gave you and <u>who lives within you</u>?*

Romans 8:9 → *You're no longer dominated by your sin-bent flesh, but now you're led by the Holy Spirit, <u>who lives in you</u>.*

Ok, so let's get real here: Do you really believe that God's Holy Spirit lives within you? Because if you don't, then how is God going to talk to you, or empower you with inner strength through his Spirit? Try to answer that question.

You might be thinking, *"I just don't feel God's Spirit in me. Not at all! Is something wrong with that?"*

Nope. It takes a bit of faith to believe this as fact...but here's the thing→ We know God doesn't lie. If he says his Spirit lives in us, then we just need to believe it.

"But aren't I supposed to feel something?"

Let me ask you something. Can you feel your blood flowing throughout your body? No. But you know that it's happening, otherwise you'd be dead. You kind of accept it by faith, right? It's the same for God's Spirit. He's living in you, infusing you with spiritual life that flows through you. It's what makes you spiritually alive. Without him, you'd be spiritually dead. And, just as you accept the fact that your blood flows through you making you alive physically, accept the fact that God's Spirit flows through you making you alive spiritually.

Get this → Jesus said to a man who brought his son to be healed: *"Anything is possible if a person will just believe."* The father's response was awesome: *"I do believe, but help me overcome my <u>un</u>belief."*

Why can't we be open with God like that? Sometimes I think we feel we need to be perfect little children in front of our heavenly Father, otherwise he'll be displeased with us. Perhaps that comes from living in such a performance-based society. One of my favorite prayers is, *"God show me my heart and what you want to change in me."* Whenever I pray that, I smile because it's not long before he does...and what I see...well, it's not pretty.

Day 44 → Get Used To It

Psalm 23:4 → *Even when I walk through dark valleys in my life* (feeling unsafe, unsure, not knowing what's ahead), *I will not be worried or afraid* (a faith choice), *for you are close beside me and your shepherd's staff protects and guides me.*

That is a very confident statement by the writer of that verse about knowing that God is right there beside him, guiding him and protecting him. He knows nothing's going to shake him.

You know what we need to do? We need to get used to the idea that we live on planet earth and we're going to have troubles, even it's not our fault. If we can accept that, then the next thing we need to decide on is what we're going to do *while* we're in the middle of the trouble. Are we going to be worried or afraid? Or, are we going to be confident like the writer of that verse above?

Take a look at this verse:
James 1:2 → *When you run into a lot of problems, or encounter a bunch of trouble and trials, consider it a joy, because it's going to challenge your faith. And when you make it through the trouble, still holding onto your faith, you'll be even stronger when more trouble comes down the road.*

Do you see those two words - *"consider it"*
That's the choice we have to make. How are we going to consider the situation we're in? Are we going to look at our crummy circumstances as a chance to let God teach us something and grow from it...or...are we going to complain and be inwardly angry at God for letting that bad stuff happen to us?

If God allowed an accident to occur in your life and you lost your leg, how are you going to consider it? You could complain and be angry at God, or you could surrender the situation to him and allow him to make lemonade out of the lemons in your life.

If you think about it, the choice is only ours to make. - *"Consider it"*

> *Nothing is permanent in this world, not even our troubles.*
> Charlie Chaplin

🌳 Day 45 → What If We Knew This Promise By Heart?

1 Peter 3:12 → *God notices and pays attention to those who <u>continually do what is right before him</u>. And, because of this, his ears are <u>attentive to their prayers</u>.*

Sometimes I think that people expect God to automatically hear their prayers, irrespective of how they are living their lives. But that verse above might make us want to check our lifestyle to see if we're <u>continually doing what's right before his eyes</u>, especially if we want him to hear our prayers.

I'm not pointing a finger. This verse simply jumped out at me when I was reading the Bible about prayer one day.
It never dawned on me that God might have some requirements if he's going to listen to our prayers.

So, here's the deal:
Wanna know how we can <u>guarantee</u> that God will hear our prayers? It's right there in that verse. Just continually make the choice to live as he tells us to, by <u>continually doing what's right before his eyes</u>.
It's a promise, just like that verse says. He'll pay attention to our requests.

Want to know a good way for God *not* to hear our prayers?
That's right. → <u>Continually *don't* do what's right before his eyes</u>.

You're probably one who has no problem living as God wants us to. But there are many believers who struggle with that. I think it's important to remember that God, as our heavenly father, gives us rules to follow, not to make life hard for us, but to protect us from messing up our lives. He's just trying to keep us in the sphere of his blessings. He knows what will hurt us or help us.

Too often we waver with our walk. Sometimes we obey and sometimes we follow our own desires. But one thing is for certain, if we hang around God a lot, we'll start to think and act as he does. And guess what? It becomes easy for us to continually do what is right. That, my friend, is an open door for God to hear our prayers.

<u>Doing what's right today means no regrets tomorrow.</u>   Keith Kellog

Day 46 → Taste and See For Yourself

Psalm 34:8 → *Taste and see, try it and find out for yourself that God wants to give you good things (Hebrew meaning- to give you good things that are pleasant, that will help you thrive and prosper and do well in life).*

That's what we have to do…we have to <u>taste it</u> and <u>try it out</u>…with faith in what God says, otherwise, how are we going to find out and experience the good things of God?

Some of us may be thinking, *"Well I follow God and I don't see myself prospering or doing well in life."*

I get it, but it's God the creator of the universe who's making promises like this to us. So, who are we to argue with him? If he wants to give us good things, who are we to doubt it.

Here's a question for us → **If we're *not* seeing these blessings happening in our lives**, then what is it that we might be missing? Because God's ready and waiting. My answer is pretty basic: If we do the things God tells us to, then we are <u>guaranteed</u> all the wonderful things God promises. Plain and simple. He never lies and he never fails to deliver on his promises.

So, we need to do a heart-check. Are we doing what he tells us to do? If not, then start, and then get ready to taste and see. Get ready to find out. Keep reminding God that you're expectantly waiting for all those great things he said he would do. He won't let you down. God's timing is always perfect.

You know, one of the reasons God wants to bless us is so the world at large would see how good he is. He says so in his Word. He wants us to taste and see how good he is so that others can see it as well. If the world sees impoverished Christians just struggling to make it in life, what does that say about God?

Live in such a way that if people should see you, they would see the goodness of God in your life.

Day 47 → Use Your Flashlight

It's been said that life is a journey, not a destination. That journey is a path that can have twists and turns and a lot of rocks and bumps to trip us up. God's Word can make the journey much smoother and safer. Check out this promise:

Psalm 119:105 → *Your Word God, is a flashlight to my feet and a spotlight to my path.*

Have you ever traveled in the darkness of night on a path strewn with rocks, with no light to help you along the way? I have, many times during our summers up in Maine. It's tricky not to stumble. But with a flashlight, it makes the going so much faster and easier.

Having a strong light that can shine far ahead is also helpful if we want to see what direction our path is taking us. If we're going to succeed on the sometimes-bumpy path to success, we need the guidance of God's Word to keep us from tripping or stumbling or going the wrong direction that leads to problems.

Is that verse above a promise of God? Sort of. How could we use it? Instead of reminding God, we can just declare it; something like this: *"It's a promise of God that his Word will make me wise (See Psalm 19:7). And, because I'm careful to follow his Word, I receive the wisdom and direction it gives me so I won't trip up or go astray."*

God has made it a law in this universe that light always dispels darkness. That's fascinating to me. Darkness can never ever overcome light. If we're in a dark part on our journey through life then we better grab God's flashlight and start using it so we can find our way and not trip or fall. God is in the light.

> God is light and in him is no darkness…at all. 1 John 1:5

The light of God's love will pierce even the darkest night.

Day 48 → Fruity…Yum Yum!!!

John 15:8-11 Jesus speaking→ *My father in heaven is glorified and honored when you produce much fruit. I have loved you just as my father in heaven has loved me. So, remain in my love. (Here's how) When you obey my instructions, you remain in my love, just as I obey my father's instructions and thus remain in his love.*
*I have told you these things so that **my joy** will be in you and that **your joy** may be full.*

Go backwards in this verse. → Notice two joys are mentioned here. One is Jesus' joy and the other is our own joy. Why are there two joys mentioned?
One answer is that we need lots of things that come from God himself in order to survive this life – things like his joy, his peace, his strength, his hope, etc. Without his traits operating in us, it's practically impossible to live the life God wants for us on our own.

There are two other things in that verse above that are worth mentioning if we want to have joy and be able to keep it. Did you catch them?
       1) producing much fruit.   **2)** remaining in his love.

In that verse, Jesus said he mentioned those two things '*so that*' we would have *his joy* within us and *our own joy* would be full? Those two words '***so that***' are important. Why? Because you need to produce much fruit and remain in his love '*so that*' you can have *his* joy

Well…how do we get joy from being fruitful or remaining in his love?
Well if you think about it, whenever we're productive and accomplishing things in our lives, it usually gives us satisfaction and joy, right?
It's the same way in God's kingdom. → When we're producing fruit (not just some fruit…but '*much*' fruit), it will give us joy.

Now, combine that with being in the center of his love (remaining in his love) by spending time with him, you can imagine it will lead to a lot of joy.

Fruitfullness is not the ultimate goal. Faithfulness is.

🌳 Day 49 → How Do We Learn To Trust God?

One way is <u>seeking to know him</u>, out of a hunger to experience him. If you're not hungry for God, you probably won't seek to know him. And if you don't know him very well, you probably won't really trust him that much.

It's hard to trust a total stranger, and it's even harder to trust someone we only kind of know. But most of us will trust someone with the important things in our lives if we really know them well. Trust is won, not given. Has God won your trust?

The only way we're going to truly trust God with the important things in our lives is to get to know him intimately. And that will only happen when we diligently, carefully, and consistently <u>seek</u> to know him.

Wanna know how God wants us to live? That's right…Trusting him. Take a look at this verse below:

<u>Galatians 2:20</u> → *It is no longer just me living my life, but Christ is living within me, and the life I now live in this earthly body of mine, I live by faith, by <u>trusting</u> in Christ, the son of God…*

What would that look like in your life? Are you just living life, just putting up with whatever comes your way? I can tell you from experience, it's easy to do. Or, are you trusting Jesus with the little and big things that happen throughout the day, inviting him into the middle of it all, expecting him to do great things? That makes it more exciting, doesn't it?

Once I started doing that, life became much more enjoyable. I began seeing amazing things happen to me that I can only attribute to God. There's something fun about letting go of the reins and sitting back to watch God move on your behalf, wouldn't you agree?

We only have one life, and one body to live this life in. So, are we going to live as though we believe Christ is living with us, up close and personal?

<u>Christ is not just working on us but with us and through us</u>. B. Wilcox

Day 50 → Your Daddy...My Daddy

Did you know that God's desire to bless us with good things is even greater than a parent's desire to bless their own children? Look at this guarantee:

Matt 7:11 Jesus speaking → *If you, as messed up, flawed humans, know how to give good things to your children, then how much more will your father in heaven give good things to those who ask him for them?*

Two things worth mentioning here.
1) Notice the word "more". In the Greek, it's a quantitative word with the connotation of, '*How much more in quantity and with good intention will God give good things to his children than even you as parents give to your own kids?*'

2) Notice the word "ask". Even Jesus is suggesting that we ask for good things. You might think that it's selfish to do so. But, the reality is that if you don't ask then you won't receive.
Plus, it robs God of the chance to make his children happy, just like any parent wants.

Has your child (if you have one) ever asked you for good things? Doesn't it feel good and make you happy to give it to them? Well, you're now a child of royalty and the king is your heavenly Father...so start asking.

Some of us feel that it's selfish to desire good things in our lives, but I think that desire was built into us by God. If you think about the first two humans God made, he provided them with really good things → a comfortable, beautiful, peaceful place to live, plenty to eat. There was no fear or danger anywhere they went. It was paradise! God took really good care of them. He hasn't changed. He's still the same.

I think we need to get used to the idea that, just as that verse above says, God wants to give us really good things. If you believe that, then start to receive them from your loving heavenly Father. Open your hands wide and take it in. He's only acting like any loving father would...only more so because he's perfect.

__Life is God's gift to us. What we do with it is our gift to God.__
A.R. Bernard

Day 51 → Wanna Know Something That's Strange?

Many people think God doesn't want them to have good things in their lives and that if he even blesses them at all, then he'll be stingy about it. They think that he'll be annoyed with them if they ask him for more. They think God's only pleased when they only have just enough, barely enough to get by…. "*After all,*" they say, "*that's not what life's about.*"

But, that's not what God's about. All through the Bible we find God expressing his desire to lavish upon his *obedient* children more and more blessings to make life good for them…more than they could possibly imagine.

You know what? God wants us to enjoy life, enjoy each other, and enjoy his creation. That was his original plan for us way back in the garden.

If you doubt whether God is serious about us asking him for stuff, then read this guarantee:

John 16:24 Jesus speaking→ *Ask me for things* (with faith backing it up) *and you will receive it, so that **your joy** may be full.*

What's the point of our 'asking' in this promise? → So that it will give us a bunch of joy. I know, it could sound selfish if we don't look at it the way God does, but hey, I didn't say it, the king of the universe did.

And notice that Jesus is telling us in that verse that he wants our joy to be full, not partial joy, but full of joy. Why would our joy be full? Because we're getting what we ask for. Why else would it cause us joy? Of course, having the right motives is important. That's why the Bible tells us to "*delight ourselves in the Lord and he will give us the desires our heart should have*" (See Psalm 37:4). That's how we maintain the right motives. **So start asking him for stuff.**

> *Ask God for what you want, but be willing to take what God gives you.*

🌳 Day 52 → <u>Can You Hear That Voice Behind You?</u>

<u>Isaiah 30:21</u> → *If you leave God's paths and go astray, you will hear his voice behind you saying to you, "Don't go that way, go this way."*

Notice that it's 'God's paths' not our paths that it's referring to. When we stray away from *his* paths, then it means we're walking on our *own* path. God knows that could lead to problems and that's when he steps in to protect us by speaking to us, reminding us to get back on his path.

What if we miss his voice?
That's a problem. We need to be able to hear him or we might *keep* walking down the wrong path and it probably won't be the blessing God intended, and that's what you'll miss out on.

<u>It might just be that we need to put on our spiritual hearing-aids.</u>

You might be thinking, "*I feel like I'm always in the dark. It's like I'm walking blind. I don't even know if I'm on God's paths.*"

If you feel like that, then read this promise.
<u>Isaiah 42:16</u>→ *I, God, will <u>lead</u> the blind along a path they're unfamiliar with, and I will guide them along <u>a road they've haven't traveled before</u>. I will make the darkness they're in become <u>light</u> and I will make the <u>rough paths into smooth terrain</u>. This is what I will do for them. I will not abandon those who are mine.*

Are you God's child? Then, that verse is directed to you.
- If you feel like you're walking blindly, God will walk with you, leading you, protecting you.
- If you feel like you're stuck on the path you're on, God promises to lead you down a new path, one you've haven't traveled before.
- That darkness you feel you're in? God will turn it into the brightness of day (that's what the Hebrew word for 'light' means in this verse). You'll be able to see your way clearly. No stumbling.
- If you feel the path you're on is pretty rough and hard to travel on, God promises to smooth it out (the Hebrew word for '*smooth*' means to straighten it out and make it flat and easy to travel on).

<u>Not all storms come to disrupt our lives, some come to clear a path</u>.

🌳 Day 53 → Hey, I Didn't Ask For This Trouble!

You might be thinking, "*Well, what if I didn't cause the trouble I'm going through? What if it was because of...*"

Then we need to trust that God knows what's going on and that he'll work it all out for our good. **Do you believe that?**

Take a look at this guarantee God makes to us:
Romans 8: 28 → *We <u>know</u>* (Greek meaning- we are convinced of this with absolute certainty) *that if we love God, he will cause each and every detail of our lives to work together* (meaning - blended and woven together) *so <u>that it turns out for our good</u>*.

You know what that tells us? Sit back, rest, and just trust him. <u>If you're not the cause</u>, then just *'Let go and Let God'*. He says he'll work it all out to your benefit. Are you going to believe it and rest in it? Or are you going to get in the way of his plan and try to fix it yourself?

Keep in mind: It may take a little time for God to lead you out of the trouble and turn it all around, but you can be absolutely certain that he'll do it according to his plan and his timing, not yours.

It may or may not be the way you wanted it to work out, but it will always be for your good. He promises it. I mean, if you injured your arm and needed surgery, and your family was praying for a full recovery, but instead, the doctors had to remove your arm, you may not be happy about it, but are you going to know with *certainty* that God will work it all out for your benefit and his glory? That's a tough one isn't it? But that's the reality we need to live in. What we can hang our hat on is that he's madly in love with us and wants nothing but good things for us...all of the time.

> **So, whatever the end-result is, it will be good.**
> **Never forget that.**

<u>*The world can create trouble in times of peace, but God can create peace in times of trouble.*</u>

🌳 Day 54 → <u>You Know What's The Hardest Thing?</u>

<u>Waiting</u>. It's waiting for God to show his supernatural power...especially in us when we feel weak and on a losing streak.

But, here's what God promises us:

Isaiah 40:31 → Those *who patiently <u>wait</u> for God, trusting him to help them; <u>they will renew their strength</u>* (their strength will be made new again). *They will rise up and fly like an eagle. They will run and not get tired.*

The strength being renewed here is *our* strength, not God's. Yes, God infuses *his* strength into us, but this is talking about us regaining our strength. That will only happen when we relax, stop trying and start trusting...just <u>waiting</u> for God to act.

Too often we're impatient for God to work, so we start doing and doing...the complete opposite of *resting* and *waiting*. All that does is wear us out. Waiting on God means he does the work, and we rest. It renews our strength, renews our faith, renews our confidence, so we can rise and fly high above our circumstances. We can handle the marathon of life that's ahead of us.

Take a look at this instructional verse:
1 Chronicles 16:11 → *Search for God and seek <u>his</u> strength. In fact, seek his face continually.*

Part of waiting on God is resting, as I just mentioned. And part of resting is seeking God and seeking *his* strength. I find it interesting that it doesn't say for us to seek ways to make *ourselves* stronger through social media or self-help books. It says to get our strength from God, to seek *his* strength.

And, you know what? He knows exactly <u>how much strength</u> to give us. He doesn't just dish out a random amount. He's aware of our situation and he gives us just the right amount he knows we need. Isn't that amazing?

> ***<u>Worrying doesn't change anything, but trusting God changes everything.</u>***

Day 55 → What Kind Of Strength Do You Want?

Some of us might be thinking: *"I try to believe, but it's hard. I need strength to believe. It doesn't come easy for me."*

I totally understand. I'm right there with you. I wrestle with believing and trusting God for these things, just like all of us do. Sometimes it seems impossible to muster up enough strength to believe. But that doesn't change the fact that you and I need to keep trying. Don't give up.

By the way, what is it exactly that God is strengthening in us? Have you ever thought about that? I'll tell you what I think. →
When God gives us his strength, he might make us stronger physically, or emotionally, or even spiritually. It's different for all of us, but God knows what we personally need.

Isaiah 40:29 says → *God gives strength to those who feel tired and worn out. And he gives power to those who feel powerless.*

** Are you feeling worn out and tired from all the stress and worry? Having his strength in you will make you <u>physically stronger</u>

** Are you <u>mentally</u> and <u>emotionally</u> drained? His strength in you will make your your thoughts and your emotions stronger so you can handle the things you're going through.

** Are you <u>spiritually</u> feeling dry and empty? His strength in you will strengthen your faith.

Ephesians 6:10 says → *Be strong in the Lord* (meaning receive strength from him, live in his strength, make his strength your strength), *and be empowered with his power.*

Maybe some of us need to get beyond doubt and get into believing God for what he says he'll do for us. After all, is doubt any easier than believing?

> ***God gives unexpected strength when unexpected trials come upon us.*** Charles Spurgeon

Day 56 → Contingencies! What Contingencies?

I have found that when I ask people if they think God has any requirements or expectations for answered prayer, I usually get a blank face. Mostly what I get from people is that they've never really thought about it.

But, you know what? God has several <u>contingencies</u> for answered prayer. Here's one of them in the verse below:

<u>Matthew 21:22</u> Jesus speaking→ *You may ask for <u>anything</u> in prayer, and **if** you <u>believe</u> and have faith, you will receive it.*

Well what if we've asked, but no answer has come?

The key in that verse above isn't the freedom to ask for *anything* we want...it's the word '***believe***'. That's the first key.

The second key is '***motive***'. Get these two right and God will answer your prayer. That's what he says he'll do.

And if you still don't get an answer...well maybe you have.

Notice this contingency:

<u>Mark 11:24</u> Jesus speaking→ *I tell you the truth, whatever you ask for in prayer to God, believe that you have **<u>already received it</u>**, and it will be given to you.*

Don't miss that important criteria for prayer: Do you believe you've <u>already</u> received what you've asked for in prayer? If you do, then that's sure proof of your faith, isn't it?

I often find myself asking for something and then forgetting about it throughout the day. It just shows that I just wasn't serious about it, or that I had little faith that God would answer me. However, had I truly believed it was in agreement with God's will and that I had <u>already</u> received it, I doubt I would have acted that way.

> ***<u>Prayer</u>*** *– the world's greatest wireless connection.*

Day 57 → Gimme Shelter

Yeah...that's from the Rolling Stones. And I never fully liked their music (ok...some of it). ☺

If I were to ask you how you find shelter or refuge in God, what would you say? I know...it's hard to verbalize, isn't it?

One answer would be, get under his wings, because if you're right in the middle of his presence, you're safe and you can just rest, even while you're going through the trouble you're going through. **Take a look at this verse below:**

Psalm 57:1 → *Underneath your wings is where I will take refuge* (like a chick under a mother hen's wings). *There I will feel safe until the trouble passes.*

And this verse:
Psalm 91:1 → *God will cover you lovingly with his feathers and under his wings you will find refuge.*

There are many verses throughout the Bible that say the same thing. Even Jesus quoted a Psalm while sitting overlooking Jerusalem. He said, *"Jerusalem, Jerusalem, how often would I have gathered you under my wings, as a hen gathers her brood, but you would not."* (See Matthew 23:37)

Let's not be one of the '*would-nots*'. Let's get under his wings. That's the safest place to be when trouble comes our way. And, just like the first of those two verses says, let's stay there *until* the trouble passes.

I think too often we grow restless and move out from under his protective wings. We become sitting prey to that waiting fox, our enemy who wants to devour us. There's no substitute for God's wings, even if we think we'll find it in something else.

So, remember this:
The safest place on earth is being tucked right under God's wings.

Day 58 → Just Two Little Bitty Letters

One of the enemy's favorite weapons against us is just two little letters – *"If "*.

You can see the attack when Jesus was in the wilderness for forty days. → *"If you are the Son of God..."*

What was the enemy trying to do to Jesus? Get him to *doubt* God.
And, what's the enemy trying to make us do? Doubt God. → *"If God really loves you, then why does he allow…"*

But here's the thing, God does love us and he gave us the same weapon Jesus used against the enemy, *"It is written..."*

When Jesus quoted the truth of God's Word, the enemy stopped harassing him. So, that tells us it all comes down to the 'truth'. Who's really telling the truth? God? Or the evil-one? → *"If God really loves you, then why does he allow…"*

Maybe that's why we need to heed the truth in Jesus' words in the verse below:

Mathew 4:4 → *It's not just bread and food that keeps people alive, their lives depend on every word that God speaks.*

If we choose to believe God instead of the enemy, then we need to use the same weapon Jesus used against the enemy. → the *"It is written…"* weapon. That means we should know what God says in his Word and speak the truth in faith back to the enemy (whether in our heart or out loud).

But you know what? If we don't know *what* God says in his Word then we probably won't have very much faith. And if we don't have much faith in what God says, then we won't be very effective in using the *"It is written"* weapon against the enemy. That delights the enemy of our souls.

But that's not you and me. We wield that *"It is written"* weapon against the enemy, because we know the Word of God and our faith stands on it. Our very lives depend on it.

God is up to something or the evil-one wouldn't be fighting you this hard.

Day 59 → People Blame God For A Lot Of Stuff

One thing is clear, God's doesn't bring adversities, sickness or poverty. He will allow it for his own purposes, but they aren't from him. In fact, if there were no evil in this world, there would be no adversities, sickness or poverty.

God can, however, use those situations for our good and turn them into blessings. After all, God's in the business of making lemonade out of lemons. **You know this next promise:**

Romans 8:28 → *We know with certainty that for all those who love God, he causes each situation to work out for their good.*

God's blessings always bring good things, without sorrow attached to them. Take a look at this next promise:

Proverbs 10:22 → *It is God's blessings that bring wealth and prosperity and well-being to a person. And <u>he adds no sorrow to it</u>.*

Those two verses are telling us that God has no intention of making us suffer, nor to add sorrow to our lives. The enemy of our souls does, but not God. No, God has every intention of picking up the broken pieces of the messes in our lives and make something good come out of it all.
But God is never late, nor is he ever early. He's right on time…according to his timing, not ours.

The problem comes when we get impatient for God to do something. Maybe he is behind the scenes and it's just not apparent to us, that's all.

What God does expect us to do is to wait patiently for him to act, to trust in his wisdom and his timing…watching and waiting with expectancy and faith. That may be the hardest thing to do – watching and waiting for God to come through. It is for me at least. Yet I'm always amazed when he does comes through. It's usually when I don't expect it, but it always seems to be in perfect timing and always for my good. How about you?

> ***Waiting on the Lord is never wasted time.*** Charles Stanley

🌳 Day 60 → Desires Are What Drives Us

Art Buchwald once said: *The best things in life aren't things.*
How true is that? But how often do we get it wrong?
Look at this guarantee:

Psalm 37:4 → *Delight yourself in God and in his ways. Do this and he will give you the desires your heart should have.*

This is a simple promise, isn't it? If our pleasure is in God instead of making money, or increasing our possessions, or getting ahead in life, then he'll change our heart so that his desires become our desires.

Will that help us to do well in life? I think so. We won't be sidetracked with wrong desires causing us problems and complications along the way.

What's important to remember here is that God is very wealthy. His riches are immense. He does not act stingy toward his children. It's his kingdom and he wants to share it with his heirs…that's us. His desire is for us to have more than just enough. We're royalty. He's the king and we're his children. We need to live like it, don't you think?

So, you know what? We don't have to strive and struggle to make it in life. We just need to make the King the object of our desires and he'll share his kingdom with us as he sees fit.

And even when we don't seem to be prospering at this point in our lives, if we truly delight ourselves in God, enjoying his company and his way of living, then we'll be genuinely *content* all along the way.

Learning to be content with whether we have much or little is just that – a learning process. And just as the apostle Paul concluded in Romans 4, the end-result of that process should be this:

Philipians 4:13 → *I can handle anything that life throws at me because of the strength Christ Jesus gives me*

Happiness consists not in having much, but in being content with little.

🌳 Day 61 → Here's A Verse To Help Us Do Right:

I call it **The Crossroad Verse**.

Jeremiah 6:16 → *When you come to a crossroad in your life, stop* (don't go any further, don't turn left or right or even go straight ahead) *and look around* (understand where you're at…your heart, your intentions, and your motives). *Then ask for the godly way and walk in it. Travel its path and you'll find true rest and peace. But, what's your response? You refuse, saying, "No thanks. I'm not going that way. I'll go the way I want."*

There is so much wisdom in that verse on how to make right choices, it's crazy. It is my go-to verse whenever I'm tempted to do wrong. Apply it to your life and you won't go wrong either.

There are 7 points and here they are:
1) **Stop** → When you reach any crossroad (large or small) in your life, where you have to decide how you're going to proceed…stop. Don't turn to the left or the right or go any further.
2) **Look** → Understand where you're at…your heart, your intentions, and your motives.
3) **Ask** → Ask God for directions…Do I turn right? Left? Go straight ahead? He'll help you and show you the best way.
4) **Travel** → When you get the answer, travel down the path God shows you.
5) **Rest** → Check to see if you're at rest in your heart and have peace about the decision you've made.
6) **Don't Refuse** → Don't say, *"No thanks. I'm not going that way. I'll go the way I want."*
7) **Repeat** → Practice these steps until they are second nature to you.

Proverbs 3:6 → Search for God's will in all that you do, and he will show you the right path you should take.

Saint Agustine said: "*O Lord, help me to be pure, but just not yet.*" Isn't that the way we are? No? Well then, maybe it's just me. ☺ But seriously, if we just lived by this Crossroads verse, we would make our lives soooo much easier.

God does not guide those who want to run their own life.

🌳 Day 62 → God's Word = Joy

Jeremiah 15:16 → *I listened to your words carefully and they brought joy to my heart and made me very happy, because I've been called by your name.*

It's not just being in his presence that God promises us joy.... it's also in his words. I don't know if you experience this, but reading God's Word brings a lot of people joy.

If we're struggling with enjoying his Word, it could be a couple of things:
1) Some Bible translations, like the King James Version, are super hard for many people to grasp. I have nine years of university education and I scratch my head when I read it. I mean think about it. It's written in a language a few hundred years old. We don't even speak like that anymore, so it's hard to read.
Pick a translation that speaks to your heart. That's where God speaks to us...on the heart-level.

2) Speaking of heart-level, do a heart-check. If we're truly honest with ourselves, maybe there's something missing in our walk with God that's keeping us from enjoying reading his words or spending time with him.
Whatever we do, we shouldn't beat ourselves up. God totally understands us. Just make it right and like that verse says, get on with the joy.

I think there are times in our lives when we pick up the Bible and no matter what, nothing we read sinks in. Dare I say it just feels empty. I believe we can turn it around, though by asking the Spirit of God to help us. I'm convinced, just as the Jesus said, the Holy Spirit who lives within us will guide us into all truth. If we would ask him to reveal the truth in God's Word, he will, and we'll quickly find meaning in our Bible reading. That's why Jesus said he was sending the Holy Spirit to live inside us – so he could be our counselor, our comforter, our helper. Jesus said the Holy Spirit will only speak to us only what Jesus himself says to him. If I'm not mistaken, that means when the Holy Spirit leads us and guides us, and speaks to us...it's Jesus.

Enjoy God and you will enjoy your life.

🌳 Day 63 → *"What exactly is 'God's kingdom' anyway?"*

Glad you asked.→ The kingdom of God, in the Bible, is simply the realm in heaven and on earth where God reigns and his will is done. Of course, there's more to it than that, but that's a foundation point on which all the rest is built.

Every kingdom has a king, and the king God appointed for his kingdom is his anointed one, the risen Christ. Jesus has been *'appointed and anointed'* to be our king. (Sorry, I just liked the way that sounded.☺). And any king has loyal subjects...us.

So, we need to decide who is going to be king in our lives - God or us? After all, if we're going to seek God's kingdom, then ultimately, he has to be the king...not us. And if he's king in our lives, then our allegiance must go to what pleases him, not just what pleases us.
Luckily for us, we don't have to figure out what he wants. It's all written out for us. Just seek out and follow the King's instructions in his Word.

One other thing about 'seeking his kingdom':
God's kingdom is filled to the brim with blessings and good things. It's a fun place to be, when you seek his kingdom, it's ok to seek those blessings as well. God had you in mind when he made those good things. In his kingdom, it's all good→ wisdom, protection, healing, prosperity, abundant joy, laughter, fun, peace, happiness etc. It's all for his loyal subjects – us.

So, here's what I want you to remember:
 If you want to seek God's kingdom, here are 4 steps that will help:
SEEK = Set + Elect + Expect + Keep
1) **Set** your desires and attentions on finding God's kingdom and his kingship...not yours.
2) **Elect** him to be king in your life and take yourself 'off' the throne.
3) **Expect** all the other things you've been striving for to be provided and worked out by your king.
4) **Keep** the king's orders (living the way he tells us to in his Word) so he can keep you safe and bless you with good things.

When we seek the Kingdom of God, the natural becomes supernatural.

🌳 Day 64 → It's Not That Hard, Is It?

Let me point something out that's crucial here in order for God's promises to come true in our lives:

God makes it crystal clear what he expects of us. To pay attention to his voice, to listen to his instructions and continually do them. That's what will open the door for him to bless us. He says it many times, over and over again, so we don't miss it. So... guess what? That's what we need to do.

Always remember → His instructions aren't there to keep us under his thumb. They are there to help us avoid ruining our lives. They are there to help us *stay* in his sphere of blessings.

Some of us might be saying, *"But, it's just too hard!"*
Take a look at these promises:

1 John 5:3 → *Loving God means doing what he tells us to do, and really, his instructions are not burdensome or hard for us at all.*

Mathew 11:30 Jesus speaking → *The burden that I ask you to bear is easy to carry, and all that I require of you is easy to do.*

Proverbs 10:22 → *God's blessings will make you happy and help you to advance and prosper in life, without painful toil for it.*

What are these verses promising us? → That doing what he tells us to do is not hard...at all.

So then why is it so hard for us to just do it?
I personally think we can get so distracted with life that God Word gets shoved in the corner of our day...something we'll get to when we have the time. Instead of making it a priority in our lives, something we look forward to, it becomes a burden, something we have to do or else we'll feel guilty.
Now I know that's neither you nor I, but sometimes we can get pretty close to feeling that way, don't you think?

Personally, I have adhered to the following verse and I believe God has blessed me for it. He'll bless you as well...if you do it. Here it is:
Psalm 119:147 → *I will rise up early in the morning and seek you, God.*

God's makes his way of living easy...but we seem to make it hard.

Day 65 → Money...Money...Money!!!

Zig Zigler once said, "Money can't make you happy...but everybody wants to find out for themselves.

If that's you, then here are a few warnings, and if you heed them, they will save you a lot of time and discouragement in your path to finding God's blessings and prosperity:

Look at this verse:
Luke 16:11 Jesus speaking→ *If you've not been shown to be trustworthy with your worldly wealth and possessions, then how can you be trusted with the true riches of heaven?*

God wants to trust us with his true riches which will always bless other people as well as ourselves. But he knows he can't do that if we're not faithful with what he's given us in our lives, our jobs and our businesses.

What are the true riches of God?
They're spiritual in substance, riches that will last for eternity - like wisdom, true understanding, protection from evil, prosperity, happiness, joy, peace, and the list goes on.
All of these come from the wealth and possessions of God. They are what the Bible calls "gold and silver", compared to temporal earthly riches and accomplishments that it calls "wood, hay, and dust". Can God trust you and I with his true riches?

So, what does God want us to do?

Matthew 6:19 Jesus speaking → *Don't just accumulate riches and possessions in your earthly life, where they can break down, or be stolen. Instead accumulate true riches for yourself in heaven where they will last forever and never lose their value.*

All of us have to make a choice. What are we going to accumulate in our lifetime. **Which will it be for you?**

In this world we live in, it's not what we gather up, but what we give up, that makes us rich.

🌳 Day 66 → <u>According To Our Faith</u>

<u>2 Corinthians 5:7</u> → *The way we live this life* (as followers of God) *is by <u>faith</u>* (by believing God and what he says), *not by how things may appear to us.*

Do you remember Jesus saying to the leper, "Your <u>faith</u> has made you well again." (See Luke 17:11).

And to the blind man, "*According to your <u>faith</u>, see again.*" (See Mathew 9:29)

It was their faith that caused God to respond, right? So, what does that tell us we need to do? → Speak out God's promises with *faith* in our words.

After all, God says his promises will always accomplish what he intended, and what brings those promises to life in our lives is our *faith* in what God said he would do.

Some of us may be thinking: *"Yeah, well, I tried declaring God's promises God and my problems are still here. It didn't work for me."*

Wait a second. The trouble you're experiencing doesn't change the Word of God. It's still the same. So, don't give up on his promises.
Don't let your circumstances change your faith, let your faith change your circumstances.

<u>Lamentations 3:25</u> says that '*God is good to those who wait for him to act.*' In the Hebrew language, the meaning of the phrase <u>God is good</u> means he'll come through with good things so that it will help us when we need it. God has every intention of making our lives better. That includes helping us with our troubles. But it often involves waiting for his goodness to happen…and that takes faith, right?

And just as that verse says at the top of the page, it's the way we live that matters. In other words, we're supposed to walk through each day dependent on God's wisdom, his goodness, his timing, his abilities, and his power in all the circumstances we encounter. In other words — we're to live each and every day by…*faith*.

In the end, we only regret the chances we didn't take → Live by faith.

Day 67 → <u>Singing?... Really</u>?

<u>**Psalm 95:1&3**</u> → *Sing with <u>joy</u> to the Lord.*
<u>**Psalm 84:2**</u> → *My heart sings for <u>joy</u> to the living God.*
<u>**Psalm 100: 2**</u> → *Enter God's presence with <u>joyful</u> singing.*

You know what these verses have in common? → Singing. Why is that? Why is there a bunch of singing going on around God all the time? Doesn't he like some peace and quiet up there?

Maybe it's because he likes music. Or, maybe it's because music is the quintessential organized expression of all that is orderly in God's universe, and thus it is the fitting expression toward God.

Music's core is based in mathematics. It just looks different. It's like the equivalent of a mathematical formula, only melodic in structure.

I don't know about you, but what those verses are talking about doesn't come easy for me. There are over a hundred Bible verses that talk about singing to God, so I guess I better get used to it.

All I can say is that in God's presence there's a lot of joy and it probably leads to a lot of singing. So, it's probably good for us to express that feeling back to God.

In other words, joy seems to be a 2-way process.→ God promises us the fullness of joy when we get in his presence, and we express it back to him in some form...like singing. I just hope he has earplugs if he hears me howlin away.

I hear people say, when they get to heaven they'll be happy to just sit at Jesus' feet and sing praises for ever and ever. Really?. I'm looking forward to that as well. But me? I want to explore God's universe. I want to learn new hobbies. I want to try new things. Maybe everyone should have a bucket list when they go to heaven. Jesus has been spending a lot of time preparing heaven for us, so he probably has a lot of amazing things for us to enjoy. I bet singing is just one of them.☺

> *<u>I am filled with an abundance of joy because of you, oh God. I will sing praises to your name.</u>* Psalm 9:2

Day 68 → Hold On To This Promise

Psalm 84:11 (last part of the verse) → *God will not hold back or refuse to give any good thing to those who continually do what is right before him*.

This is so important that we can't miss this if we want God's blessings to be poured out on our lives. → What would hold back God from letting good things flow into our lives? I'm sure you've got the answer already, but it's worth repeating. -- Not doing what God tells us to do.

I think we always need to keep in mind that doing what God tells us to is peppered all through the Bible and is deeply entwined with him blessing us. So, if you're struggling with this issue of obedience, take care of it asap so it doesn't become a '*roadblock*' to blessings.

Remember this → When God tells us to do stuff in his Word, he's giving us boundaries and protection.→ Protection? From what? From ourselves...and from the enemy of our souls. It won't matter how much he blesses us if our desires for self-satisfaction cloud the motives of our heart. Right?

And remember this as well, God blesses us because of *his* faithfulness, not just ours. You probably aren't in rebellion against God right now, but we all seem to give in to periods of self-indulgence every now and then, where we put our '*self*' first, instead of God.

And, you know as well as I do, when we act like badly behaved children, then, God, because he loves us so much, just might put us in the corner...with no dessert, so to speak....in other words, no blessings.
But, as soon as we turn back to him and get back on his path, we find him waiting to do us good again. So, you know what I say? → *Stop messin' with the blessin'*. Stay in God's favor.

God is more interested in our character than he is in our comfort.

🌳 Day 69 → Humongous, Mammoth, Elephantine

How would you like to have a huge amount of peace as you walk through life; not just a bit of peace that comes and goes, but a humongous, mammoth, enormous, elephantine, gargantuan amount of peace. Check out the guarantee below:

Psalm 119:165 → *Those who have a passion for God's instructions will have great peace (a huge amount of peace). Nothing will cause them to stumble and fall in their walk through life.*

With a promise like this how can we go wrong? Would you agree? Ok, you're right. I forgot.→ It can go wrong...really wrong for us. There will be a bunch of stumbling and falling going on as we struggle through life **if** we don't have a desire for his instructions.
In fact, the Hebrew word for '*stumble*' literally means '*roadblock*'.

If we want to remove the roadblocks in the pathways of our lives and have a humongous amount of peace just permeating through us, then, we need to develop a passion for God's instructions on how to live our lives and then follow through with doing them. After all, he's the King and we're his loyal and faithful subjects, right? Passion for God's Word is not a gift...it's a choice.

And as a result...we'll get a huge amount of peace added into the mix. That's right. Great amounts of peace will fill our lives when we have a passion for God's Word. **Why is that?** Well, when we get to know his Word and follow it, we are nestled in God's will and favor. We were made to obey him so it will keep us in his sphere of protection and blessings. We're fulfilling God's desire for us and this brings us peace...peace with God and peace with ourselves.
It's almost a supernatural miraculous thing that happens.
We come to know with certainty that God has a heart for us to win in this life, and through obedience to his Word, we're helping to make that happen. We're cooperating with God and that brings us peace.

> *A passion for God is the most attractive feature a person could possess.*

Day 70 → God Doesn't Have To Give Us Anything.

Did you ever think about the idea that God doesn't have to give us anything? He doesn't owe us anything. Yet, he constantly tells us throughout the Bible that he wants to pour out good things on our lives.

An old country proverb says: *"Happy are those who see beautiful things where other people see nothing."*

A thankful heart does that.

We live in a society of consumers. Getting ahead means getting more…more stuff. Yet we have more than most people on the planet.

Are we thankful for our refrigerator? How about our showers and running water. We can wash our clothes with the press of a button, not rubbing them on a rock and hanging them to dry. We can turn on electricity at a whim. We can keep ourselves cool when it's too hot and warm when it's too cold. We can get in our cars and travel a few miles in a few minutes, where for others it would take hours. Yet are we thankful to God for these comforts or do we take them for granted?

We need to remember to be thankful and express our <u>thanks</u> to God when he does bless us with the little and big things, right?

<u>Psalm 50:23</u> → *The person who offers up the <u>sacrifice</u> of thanksgiving to me, that person glorifies me.*

Notice the word '<u>sacrifice</u>' in that verse. It means to give up something for the sake of another. Does God need our thanks or the glory? Nope. He knows that it's more beneficial to us than him if we do it.

Why is that?

Well, if you think about it, what are we sacrificing when we offer up thanks? We're giving up a little bit of our time, a little bit of our 'self-centeredness' (because we're giving God the credit, not us) and a little bit of our comfort zone.

So, I guess it's true: *Gratitude is the best attitude to have.*

It's not happiness that brings us gratitude. It's gratitude that brings us happiness.

Day 71 → Anybody Need A Heart-Check?

Mathew 6:33 Jesus speaking→ *So, instead, focus your attention on seeking God's kingdom above everything else in your life, and seek the right way to live that he prescribes. Do this and <u>all</u> the other things you need and strive for <u>will be provided</u>.*

This is where we all need to do a heart-check.→ *"Am I doing those things?...seeking God's kingdom first in my life, above everything else? And, am I paying attention and being careful to walk in God's ways? Or, is the daily grind and distractions of life just consuming me, keeping me from doing it?"*

If that's a struggle you're encountering...then it would behoove you to fix it. Jesus wouldn't have mentioned the importance of seeking God's kingdom over 100 times if it wasn't important.

Some of us may be thinking, *"I don't get it. What does it even mean to <u>'seek his kingdom'</u>?"*

You're not alone. When I've asked believers how they personally seek God's kingdom, many of them fumble for words. They aren't sure. **So, let me make this short and sweet:**

The Greek meaning for the word "**<u>seek first</u>**", in the verse we're talking about is this → To crave something so badly that nothing's going to get in the way of us seeking it. And until we find it, we just won't be satisfied. That's what's meant by '<u>seeking God's kingdom first</u>' in our lives.

Look at it this way: Whatever we spend the majority of our time, our interests, and our efforts on, that's what we're ultimately seeking after.

How is it with you? Is the Kingdom of God your primary aim? Again, you may need to do a heart-check with real honesty to figure this one out. I have to do it constantly, in my own life. I can easily get distracted and within no time I'm off on a tangent. But, like I said, if it weren't so important, then Jesus wouldn't have mentioned it so often.

> ***<u>Make God your first priority, not your last resort.</u>***

Day 72 → How do we _seek_ God?

<u>Diligently</u> = to apply effort, to work at it with attention and persistence.
<u>Consistently</u> = not sporadically, but regularly, in an organized fashion.
<u>Carefully</u> = the word means full-of-care.

It doesn't mean to randomly open your Bible and point your finger to any verse or turn on YouTube and watch any sermon that just shows up (although I do believe God can use those methods to reach us). It means to put some thought into it, to use some care.

Ok, you may not like me after this, but I think we all need to avoid taking the easy path and instead, buckle down and really study God's Word. After all, the Word is God speaking to us, right?

God says if we diligently seek him that way, he promises we'll find him and get to know him. Simple as that.

Some of us may be thinking, _"Well, I try to seek him, but he just seems so far away. It feels impossible to know him."_

Take a look at this <u>guarantee below</u>:
Deuteronomy 4:29 → _If you seek God with <u>all</u> your heart_ (diligently, carefully, and consistently, out of hunger to know him), _you <u>will</u> definitely find him and come to know him._

Notice, it doesn't say we _'may'_ find him. No, it says we _'will'_ find him...as long as we seek him with <u>all</u> of our hearts.

Plus, God says that he'll <u>reward</u> us for it. Look at this guarantee:

Hebrews 11:6 → _God rewards those who diligently seek him._

What is the reward? I'm not sure, but it must be good, because a reward from God is always good. The Greek meaning of that word _"reward"_ is to pay the person their wages for their hard work. God's saying, if you put in the hard work of studying my Word, you will be paid your wages. In other words, you'll definitely receive your reward.

> _**All things are difficult before they are easy.**_ Thomas Fuller

Day 73 → Sink or Swim…Or Walk On Water

When you go to God for help and the help doesn't seem to come very quickly…if at all, don't say, *"Well, I guess we just never know what God's going to do."* Yes we do. God is not obscure with his Word. Take a look at the promise below:

Isaiah 45:19 God speaking→ *I, God, do not hide my words. No, I make bold promises, not hard to understand proclamations. I only speak what is true and reliable and right.*

God doesn't mince his words. He means what he says. So, take him at his word. What he says he will do…he'll do.
Remember **1 Kings 8:56**? → *Not one word has failed in all the wonderful promises God gives.*

Agreeing with God's Word isn't always easy. It's a matter of choosing to believe what he says and acting on it over and over again, even if it seems crazy. And by doing that, guess what happens? It gets easier. That's what God means when he says in **2 Corinthians 5:7** → *"We walk through each day by faith, not by how things may appear to us."*

Do you remember the story of the apostle Peter walking on water? He was doing fine until he started sinking. What caused him to sink? He saw the wind whipping up the waves and he became afraid. He went from bold faith (acting on Christ's invitation to join him on the water) to being afraid…and then sinking. But it wasn't the raging wind or the violent waves that defeated him…it was his fear. He took his eyes off of Jesus. He looked at his circumstances and gave in to fear. The result? → Defeat.

Don't let that happen to you. Don't take your eyes off the Promise-Giver, only to focus on your circumstances. Faith and doubt never will enjoy each other's company. They're like oil and vinegar.
Pray with faith. Believe God for the answer. Thank him for what he's going to do. And wait and watch with expectancy. → That's faith.

If you only pray only when you're in trouble…you're in trouble.

🌳 Day 74 → This Ship Is Going Down!

Some of us might be thinking, *"Look, I get that there's some weird spiritual battle going on, but I've got some real-life battles happening here. I need some real-life strength or else this ship is going down!"*

Well, here's the kind of strength God's promises you:
   Take your pick.

- Emotional Strength
- Physical Strength
- Mental Strength
- Spiritual Strength

Take a look at the guarantee below:

1 Thessalonians 3:3 → *God is faithful to his Word. He'll always do what he says he'll do, and he says <u>he will strengthen you</u> and protect you from evil.*

So, are we going to hold God to his word? Are we going to fully expect him to strengthen us?

I don't know about you, but I often catch myself praying for something and then forgetting to watch for the answer. I kind of let the distractions of the day take over. I let the ball drop in expecting and waiting to see what God's going to do. That's a no-no. That won't help things.

If you catch yourself doing the same thing, get back on track and keep reminding God of his promises and wait with expectancy.

I think sometimes it's hard to muster up the faith to expect God to come through. It takes work to hold God to his word.

But faith isn't having the strength to go on – it's going on <u>when you don't have the strength</u>. It's expecting God to give you *his* supernatural strength, not to rely only on your own strength.

<u>I asked for strength and God gave me difficulties to make me strong.</u>

🌳 Day 75 → Our part comes down to one thing

Look at all that God promises to do for us, and then look at our responsibility. Our part really comes down to <u>one thing</u> – *Believing*

There's no room for whining if we cling to God's promises. He made it super easy for us. He does all the work and all we have to do is...*believe*.

So, why does it seem so hard to *believe*?

The question isn't whether we can or can't believe, but whether we're <u>*willing*</u> to believe.

The thing about faith is it doesn't require special knowledge or abilities. All of us can lay hold of faith and <u>*decide*</u> to live by it. As far as God's concerned, the <u>only</u> way to live is by faith.

Remember this verse? **2 Corinthians 5:7** → We live our lives by faith, not by how things appear.

Look at the Israelites and their 40 years in the wilderness. God had promised them protection and amazing blessings if they would just *believe* what he said and *do* what he told them to do. But what kept them from an amazing abundant life of blessings and protection? Their <u>*unwillingness*</u> to trust God and believe what he promised. They <u>*weren't willing*</u> to fight for and suffer to attain those promises he offered.

Some people may think it's foolish to blindly put our faith in the promises of God, but unless we're willing to do so, we'll never experience the many wonderful things God says he'll do for us.

So, which would you rather do? Doubt and receive nothing? Or, believe and receive all that your creator offers you – wonderful blessings.

It all comes down to...<u>*willingness*</u>. And the only one who can decide that for you is...yourself.

Faith is not believing God can. It's believing God will.

Day 76 → By-products

Did you know that joy (deep-seated happiness) is a by-product of trusting God?

Psalm 40:4 → *There is joy* (meaning - inner happiness and contentment) *for those who* truly *trust the Lord*.

If that promise is true, then there should be *joy* in our hearts as a result of our trusting God, right? How would that look in our life? I would say that inner happiness and contentment are good descriptions. Why?
Because when we take the load off our shoulders and put it on God's shoulders, trusting him to carry our burdens and to take care of things, we feel lighter, happier, and even content, knowing we don't have to worry about it anymore.

Here's another by-product of trusting God. - Strength

Isaiah 40:31 → *Those who put their trust in the Lord and wait for him to act will renew their strength. They will soar above their circumstances like an eagle and run the race without getting tired.*

The Hebrew meaning for the words '***wait for him to act***' infers patience. It infers resting and just waiting on God to do his thing, not to try to do something on our own to fix it...just wait.

That word '***renew***' in the Hebrew means 'to make strong *again*'. Do you remember times in your life when you felt strong, when you felt on top of the world, that nothing could knock you down? That's the meaning behind the word '*renew*' in that verse.

How's that gonna happen? By trusting God with everything in your life – the good, the bad and the ugly.

What will the result be? The burden will be lifted. You'll feel like you could soar like an eagle, like you could run a marathon and not get tired. You get the idea, don't you.

Waiting for God's timing is not the same as doing nothing. C.Stanley

Day 77 → Whose The Contractor Here?

Psalm 127:1 → *Unless God is building the house, the workers are wasting their time and they labor in vain* .

Notice it's <u>both</u> the workers and God that are supposed to be working together to make things happen.

There's a physical aspect and there's a spiritual aspect to what we do in life. If we don't have both (God and us involved) we could risk being misguided and miss the blessings God wants to give us. God loves to be involved with every part of our lives. That was part of his original plan for us.

You know what I think? We've become God's family of '*maintenance people*'. We just have so many things to maintain – our home, our family, our yard, our cars, our work, our hobies etc. We're so busy maintaining stuff, we don't have any time left to maintain our own spirit. We don't have the time to let God in to be right there alongside us building our lives. But can we spiritually afford to do that?

That verse above says all we have to do is stop 'directing' all our stuff and just 'chill'. Let God get involved, inviting him into the middle of each thing we do, whether great or small.

If we do this, he might just take us places we never would have considered. The Christian life is supposed to be the Great Adventure. It should be exciting, don't you think? It should never be drudgery or boring. If you're feeling your walk with God is boring, then make a change. Test God. Challenge him to show you your heart. I guarantee that you'll be in for a wild ride. He'll put people and circumstances in your life to bring out the best and the worst in you. You'll see. I promise you, it won't be boring any longer. How do I know? Because every time I ask God to show me my heart…Yikes. It ain't pretty. It's a wild ride! But I would never want to get off the roller coaster and neither should you, because the end-result will be a life that is more like Jesus. In the end, isn't that what we all want?

<u>God doesn't just give us what we can handle; God helps us handle what we've been given.</u>

🌳 Day 78 → <u>Ever see a dad get upset when his son or daughter is getting picked on by a bully?</u>

He wants to step in and fight the battle for his child. That's what God wants to do for us when the enemy picks on us. And, when God enters the fight, he never loses...ever!
Take a look at the promise below:

<u>2 Chronicles 32:8</u> → *We have God to fight our battles for us and to help us <u>win</u>.*

It doesn't say we have God to help us *so we 'might'* win. Nope, it says,"*to help <u>us win</u>*". Remember, he's doing the fighting for us, so, what's the outcome? We win, because God always wins.

Now...speak that stuff out, whether in your heart or out loud. Either way, God hears you. Something like this: → *"God, you say, you're in the battle along with me, fighting the battle for me. And, because you always win, I know I'll win…."*

And take a look at this promise:

<u>2 Chronicles 20: 17</u> → *You won't have to fight the battle. Just <u>take up your position</u> and <u>stand there</u> and <u>watch</u> God fight for you and deliver you.*

"Bam!" That's what God's Word does for us! We do our part, which is what? → Getting in a battle stance, ready to fight if we need to. **And then what?** → We watch God fight for us. Notice we're both involved. God and us. God loves to help us, but he wants to know that we're *'in it to win it'* as well.

Maybe you're not going through a battle right now, but when you do, make sure your Father in heaven is sticking up for you. He won't stand by idly when his child is being bullied by the enemy. He may want to hear you calling to him for help. He may want you to take up your position, ready to fight. Too many of us wimp-out because we didn't put God's armor on. We're not holding up our shield of faith, and when that happens...OUCH!!! Those arrows hurt!

<u>*As long as you're certain God is for you, it doesn't matter at all who's against you.*</u>

Day 79 → The Code To Blessings

Deuteronomy 6:2 → *Listen closely and be <u>careful to obey</u> the words of the Lord. If you do, <u>then **all** will go well for you.</u>*

Deuteronomy 6:23 → *The Lord God commanded us to <u>obey all of his instructions</u> and <u>to fear him</u>, **so he can continue** <u>to bless us and preserve our lives</u>.*

You know what those two verses have in common? That God wants it to go well for us, that he doesn't want anything to interfere with his blessing us and preserving our lives.
There are two things that will ensure that happening:
1) Obedience to God's instructions.
2) Living with deep respect and reverence for him.
God tells us to do these two things so that he can continue to bless and protect us. That word 'continue' is important. It's a contingency word, meaning, if we want God to continue to bless us, then do those two things mentioned above. Fear God and obey him.

People don't like the phrase *'fear of the Lord'*. It doesn't sit well with us. Probably it's based on our cultural interpretation of it. – *"You mean we should be afraid of God?"*
Well, lucky for us it has a less fearsome meaning to it in the Hebrew language.
To 'fear the Lord' in Hebrew means → *to live our lives with a deep respect, reverence, and awe of God, so much so, that it will lead to consistent obedience and godly living. All of it as a result of using serious caution and self-evaluation to avoid anything that would offend him or defame his name.*

Some of us might think, *"Well those aren't very pleasant promises."*
Actually, they're helpful to us. God has given us the <u>code</u> to a really blessed life, where things will go very well for us. Reverentially respect and obey God and you will thrive and do well in life.

Obedience allows God's blessings to flow without restraint.

Day 80 → The Secret To Contentment

Philippians 4:12 → *I have learned how to be <u>content</u> with whatever I have in life. I know how to live with almost nothing and I know how to live with almost everything. I have learned the <u>secret</u> of living in every situation I end up in.*

Why is it that we as a society at large never seem to be content with what we have? We live in a culture of accumulation. I mean, do we really need all the stuff we own? There's nothing wrong with it, but do we really neeeed it?

I think you and I need to ask ourselves this question: Are we content right where we are? If not...why not? Yes, I get it. God may have something for us that's better, but can we be content right now, where we are, until we move on to better things?

I wonder where this restlessness even comes from? Is it bred into us as a cultural norm, to the point that it seems natural to us?

And what was the secret Paul found that allowed him to just be content no matter where he was? I mean, after all, he was constantly being harangued, harassed, beaten, and whipped. If that happened to us, would we be content? Paul was not Superman. He was just like us. So, what was his secret?

Here it is. It's verse 13 → *I can handle anything that life throws at me through the <u>strength</u> that Christ gives me, through my union with him.*

That's not a very exciting answer is it? In fact it's kind of anti-climactic. But...it's the truth. That's how Paul made it through all those awful situations, still being content. He equated the strength he found in Jesus with contentment. That tells us something. We'll be content wherever we are in life because Jesus' is strengthening us inside.

<u>*Contentment isn't necessarily happiness, but happiness comes out of contentment.*</u>

🌳 Day 81 → It's Not God's Fault

Believe it or not, some believers think, *"God made this happen to me. He's the one causing this trouble in my life."*

I think those people need to remember that's not the way God works. God doesn't withhold blessings and good things from those who are careful to *do* what he tells them to.

Over and over again, throughout the Bible, he tells us of the good things he will do for his <u>obedient</u> children. And, even if we aren't obedient, God is still so kind that he spares the disobedient as long as possible, hoping they'll come back to him.

Take a look at these two guarantees below:

Exodus 34:6 God speaking → *I am God, the one who is <u>full of mercy</u> and <u>full of compassion</u>, and <u>slow to get angry</u>, who <u>shows great love</u> and <u>faithfulness</u> toward you.*

2 Peter 3:9 → *God is very, very <u>patient</u> toward us when we ignore him and go astray. He does not want any of us to be ruined or destroyed, but that we would change our ways.*

Lucky for us, God grades on the cross, not the curve, right?
1 cross + 3 nails = 4 given.

I think we all need to remember → God's heart is always for us, not against us. He wants us to do well in life...to live and prosper and enjoy his company. He doesn't want us to lose our way and get off his path. He knows the troubles it brings. That's why he gave us his instructions – to help us *stay* on the right path that leads right to his blessings.

<u>Bottom-line:</u> It's pretty simple when we think about it. → If we would just do what he says, then we'd enjoy good days. God promises it.

And remember, <u>good days</u> can still include adversity, hardship, and struggles. Think about it, how many times have we said something like this, *"Man, that was the hardest time in my life, but it was also the best."*

<u>God is always trying to give good things to us, but our hands are often too full to receive them.</u>

🌳 Day 82 → To 'Let' or 'Don't Let'...That Is The Question

Take a look at this *'Don't Let'* verse:

<u>Phil. 4:6&7</u> → *<u>Don't let</u> yourself be worried, or troubled, or fearful about anything. Instead, pray about it, telling God what you need. Then, (with faith), thank him for what he's done and is going to do. If you do this, <u>God's peace</u>, which is way beyond our understanding, will guard your thoughts from worry and your hearts from being troubled or afraid, all of it as you live your life united with Christ.*

Here's the way I see it. It comes down to <u>a choice</u> → Don't let yourself be worried...take it to God...release the situation into his hands...trust him to do what he thinks is best (regardless of what we want) and *his* peace will fill us.

And, if we start to take what was worrying us back again...that's when we need to hand it back over to God. Over and over again until it becomes less ours and more God's. Try it and see what happens. That's how we grow our faith, right?

Maybe you've heard this phrase:
When God takes the trash out, don't go digging back through it. Well, when God takes our worry, don't go taking it back again.

I think many of us forget that God is adamantly against worry. Jesus, Paul, and the apostles spoke against it. I think we treat it as an option, that we're free to worry if we choose to. But it's not an option. Nowhere in God's Word does it encourage us to worry.

So, like that verse at the top of the page says, <u>don't let</u> yourself be worried. It's all about the choice.

Besides, worry and faith don't mix well. Worry robs faith of its power.

<u>I have spent most of my life worrying about things that have never happened.</u>
Mark Twain

🌳 Day 83 → Gold, Silver, Wood, Hay, or Sawdust

1 Corinthians 3:12,13,15 → *When we stand before God, fire will reveal the value of the actions and motives of our lives – gold, silver, wood, hay or dust. And if our deeds survive, we'll be <u>blessed and rewarded</u> by God.*
But if our deeds are burned up, we'll suffer a <u>great loss</u>.

Which do you think will last through eternity? The gold and silver? Or the wood, hay and dust? Which do you think will come through the fire of God's assessment of our lives when we finally stand before him? That's right, the gold and silver. The wood, hay and dust will be burned up. It doesn't have eternal value. It's worthless in the light of eternity and what God values. It won't hold up to the fire of God's assessment.

So, you know what I think we need? We need to make sure we're faithful to God in all our endeavors in life whether work or play, from the big things to the little things…going after God's eternal gold and silver, not the temporary wood, hay and dust.

It was a turning point in my life, when I realized that most of the things I'd done in life and most of my accomplishments on this earth were nothing but wood, hay and dust. I was striving for the good life until I realized they wouldn't last; easily burned away by the fire of God's assessment of my life. It scared me to think there would be nothing of eternal value to show for my life when I stood before him. It caused me to change my priorities and choices, to invest in the eternal gold and silver, the stuff that truly matters, the stuff that will last forever.

How about you? What are you storing up for the Big Day? I think we need to do more heart-checks to examine where our motives and desires lie. If we did, we might be surprised at what lies beneath the surface. Fortunately, it's never too late to change our priorities…until our last breath.

<u>***We are where we are in life because of the choices we've made in the past.***</u>

Day 84 → You might be thinking

"Well, what if I don't have enough faith to believe what God promises?"

God understands you. He's not frowning at your unbelief. He's rooting for you. Don't forget, he's on your side. He wants you to win at life. He just happens to know that to receive his promises means you'll have to use your faith.

His promises originate in the supernatural realm, so to receive them, we have to use a supernatural method→ *'faith'*. Our faith is what releases God's Word to work in our lives. You can see examples of that all through the Bible.

Just remember this→ If we tell God our faith is weak and ask him to help our unbelief, that's exactly what he'll do. He'll put circumstances in our lives to grow our faith. We just need to cooperate with him when it happens and not avoid the hard stuff if that's part of the faith-growing process.

We were built to have faith in God. That was part of his original design of mankind. It should feel unnatural not to have faith in what God says, but since this world has been turned upside down by sin, it no longer feels *natural*. With practice, however, we can learn to live by faith each and every day. We can make it *natural* again.

Here's a good way to build up faith in your heart: → Find a promise of God that speaks to your heart and fills your need. Then, meditate on it (chew on it) and speak it over and over again through the day and week, so you're hearing it. Do this until it starts to take root in your heart. Pretty soon you'll be speaking it with faith from the abundance of your heart.

Then when those arrows of the enemy start flying, you hold that shield of faith up and speak out God's Word, just like Jesus did to the enemy, when he was tempted to give up in the wilderness.

If we want to live spiritual lives then we're going to have to do spiritual things.

Day 85 → *'In Jesus' Name...Amen and Amen'*

<u>John 16:23</u> Jesus speaking → *I tell you the truth, you can ask from God anything <u>in my name</u>, and he will give it to you.*

It's interesting to hear people end their prayer with the formulaic, *"In Jesus' Name, Amen."* In fact, it almost feels uncomfortable if we don't hear it, right?

But have you ever asked yourself why we pray in Jesus' name?
I mean, if you look at all the prayers in the New Testament, not one of them ends with the words, *"In Jesus' Name, Amen"*.

When Jesus says to ask in his name, he means for us to approach God with his authority backing us up.
When the police on TV used to say, *"Open up in the name of the law!"*, why did they say that? It's because the police were claiming their demand was backed by the authority of the government.

So, for us to ask God for something in Jesus' name, we're asking with the authority Jesus gave us to justifiably come before God with our request, since we're *in* Christ (united with him).

Jesus tells us in different ways to ask for <u>anything</u>. I think we sometimes limit God by *not* doing that. After all he wouldn't have told us over and over again to ask him for things if he didn't intend to give them to us. So, why not ask? Let's ask for the impossible. See what happens.

Here's another interesting thing: Often we pray for something over and over again, day after day, night after night. The thing is, I don't see Jesus doing that anywhere in scripture. You wanna know why I think that is? Because once he asked God for something he believed he would receive it. Could it be that we keep asking for the same thing over because we struggle to believe?

These days, when I ask God for things, I ask him and then the rest of the time I thank him for his answer as he wills it.
If you think about it, thanking God for his answer is really expressing our faith that he heard us and will answer according to what's best.

<u>If you don't ask, the answer is always "No".</u>

Day 86 → <u>Did You Know</u>?

God is thrilled to give us good things and bless us with an abundant life, right?

So, why do people blame God for terrible things happening – adversity, tragedies, calamities? *"After all,"* they say, *"if God is in control, then it must be him that caused it."*

That's not God's heart. He doesn't cause those things. He might allow them to happen for our own good, never for our destruction. **The truth is,** God repeatedly tells us of the outcome for doing what he tells us to do, and the outcome for *not* doing what he tells us to do. And then, you know what he does? → <u>He lets us choose which outcome we want.</u>

Take a look at this passage: It's sort of a promise...or...a curse.

<u>Deuteronomy 30:19&20</u> → *Today I am giving your <u>a choice</u> between life or death, between blessings or calamity. <u>It is yours to make</u>. If you choose the life I offer, it brings blessings. If you choose the path that leads to spiritual death, it will bring ruin. So, choose life. <u>You can make this choice by</u> loving the Lord your God and consistently doing what he says; sticking close by him for he is your life* (the good, abundant life your desire)...

You wanna know how God works?
1) He's God, so he makes the rules, because he knows what's best for us. His rules are designed to keep us in his sphere of blessings.
2) He tells us what to do so he can bless us, protect us, and keep us from ruining our lives.
3) If we choose to live the way he tells us to, then we can bask in the flow of his blessings.
4) If we choose *not* to live his way, then we lose out on those blessings.

    So, living God's way is a choice. Let's choose it.

<u>**Life is a matter of choices and every choice you make makes you.**</u>

🌳 Day 87 → Don't treat God like a genie in a bottle

God knows our hearts and our thoughts anyway, so we might as well get our motivation right from the very beginning, don't you think?

There's nothing wrong with wanting financial, physical, and materialistic blessings. If it were wrong, then God wouldn't have gone out of his way to mention all that he wants to do for us in those areas.

Look at what the verse below says…It's a guarantee that God will be happy when you prosper in life.

Psalm 35:27 → God takes great delight in the prosperity of his faithful servants.

I say let's do a heart-check. What's our motive in asking for what we're asking for? A Mercedes convertible or a car to get to work?

And just as that verse above says, we need to make sure we are one of his *'faithful servants'*, which means doing what he tells us to do, not necessarily what we want to do. Some of God's people don't like to think of themselves as servants, but if we want to prosper the way God wants us to, then we better be what that verse says we should be – faithful servants.

Take a look at the verse below: You could treat it as a warning and you can treat it as a promise too, if you do the opposite.

Deuteronomy 5:29 God speaking→ *Oh, if only they would have a heart like I desire; that they would listen to me and willingly do all that I tell them to do. If they did, they would prosper and everything would go well for them and their descendants.*

Can you see the need for a heart-check?

The goal God has for us → To have a heart like he desires.

Our Part → To listen and willingly do. Are we doing that?

God's Part → To prosper us and make everything go well for us.

Obeying God's vision will bring God's provision.

🌳 Day 88 → God's A Planner

Jeremiah 29:1 God speaking → *I am certain of the plans that I have for you, to give you great peace and well-being, to prosper you, not to cause harm to you. I want to give you a future that's filled with hope..*

That should bring joy to our hearts, right? God said it, so we can hold him to it. After all, wouldn't you agree he's always faithful to do what he says he'll do. *(Can I get an "Amen" to that?)* Just kidding. Sometimes I feel like I'm preaching to the choir, but this is stuff we all need to review.

We're talking about God's good intentions for us. So, take a look at the guarantee below:

James 1:17 → *Every* good gift (Greek meaning - pleasant things that make us happy and give us joy) *comes down to us from God, our father in heaven…*

Just like that verse says, God's the giver of good things. So, if you have good things in your life, chalk it up to God.

Jesus said it's the thief (the evil-one) that comes to steal those good things from us, to destroy our lives, and to kill us (see John 10:10) but that he, Jesus, came to destroy the works of evil-one, so we could have an abundant life, filled with blessings.

It's not God that makes bad things happen in our lives. It's usually Satan and his minions – the enemies of our souls. God may allow trouble to come for a good and godly reason; but usually he does not cause it...he *allows* it. God is a planner of good things, blessings that will make our lives better. Even what the devil meant for evil in our lives, God can plan good out of it. I think we need to remind ourselves of that. God's the giver of *all* good things, not bad. If we truly believe it, I think we would stop being inwardly angry at God when troubles, and adversity, and struggles engulf our lives.

When Satan knocks, say "Jesus, would you get that?"

Day 89 → Here's A Guarantee About God's Help

<u>Isaiah 41:10</u> → *Don't be anxious or worried or afraid, for I (God) am with you. And don't be discouraged, for I am your God. I will <u>strengthen</u> you (Hebrew meaning- make you stronger and support you) and I will **help** you (Hebrew meaning- come to your aid, protect you and provide for you), and I will <u>hold you up</u> by my right hand.*

Every one of those promises mentioned in that verse are meant as a blessing for us.

Why would God even bother to do those things for us? It's because he cares about us deeply in his heart and wants to make our lives easier.

What are the promises in that verse?
1) God says <u>he'll be *with* us</u>. My question is this.→ Is there anyone greater in this entire universe than God that could be with us?

2) He says <u>he is *our* God</u>. What this means is that he isn't just a statue, or an image in a church. Nope. He's alive and personal, and he wants to be intimately involved with us.

3) He says he'll make us <u>stronger</u>. In what way? → physically, mentally, emotionally, and spiritually stronger. What area do you need strength in? He'll strengthen it.

4) He says he will <u>help</u> us. How? → Any way he wants to. That's up to him. Just know it will happen and it will be to our good.

5) He says he'll <u>hold up our right hand in victory</u>.→ In the Old Testament, when God says he'll hold you up with his right hand, it was a sign of victory...that the battle is being won. And here's the thing.→ If God is <u>always</u> victorious...and I mean "always", then we'll be victorious as well. If he's our father in heaven, the creator of the universe, <u>is there anything too hard for him</u>?

If God is for us, then who can possibly overcome us?

🌳 Day 90 → Let go and Let God

So, often we miss out on what God wants to do for us <u>in</u> our troubles, because we get upset when he doesn't handle the problem the way we think he should.

And when he doesn't rescue us according to our timing, we let our faith waver. We might sulk, or give up, or get angry at God, or we might just try to do things on our own to fix the situation.

As a result, we mess up what God was trying to do in our lives in the first place...making lemonade out of lemons. So, stop messing with the blessing! No wavering or fixing it.

Some of us might be thinking → *"Wait! What are you talking about? Where's the blessing in our troubles?"*

Well, God might have plans for you to grow through your struggles. Have you thought about that?

<u>2 Corinthians 4:17 says</u> → *Our short-lived troubles only serve to help us gain an eternal glory, and that glory is far greater than our troubles.*

What glory in eternity will we have if we <u>don't</u> handle our troubles well? None. I know, I speak from experience.
I smile when I think back on how I would expect God to come through the way I wanted him to. But he decided to keep me in the trial longer than I wanted so he could teach me some stuff. Instead of accepting that, I was kind of upset with God. I sulked. I took a break from him. I'm sure he was smiling at my behavior.

But truth be told, I missed out on a lot of opportunities for growth and blessings because of my immaturity. Don't let that happen to you.
        So, again...***Stop messin' with the blessin'.***

<u>*When God gives you a "No," give him a "Thank You."*</u>
<u>*He was protecting you from less than his best*</u>.

🌳 Day 91 → <u>Hey...Where's My Blessing?</u>

God tells us he wants to meet every one of our needs and that it gives him great pleasure to prosper his obedient children. But some of his children still haven't seen the blessings and success and prosperity they desire. Why is that?

They might be thinking, *"I'm willing and waiting for it, but I don't see it happening to me?"*

The answer is that it takes more than just being *'willing'*, right? It also takes <u>consistently *'doing'* what God tells us to do</u> in <u>every</u> area of our lives. That's what's referred to in the Bible as *'obedience'*. There are many verses in the Bible about the good things from God that will come our way, if we live the way he prescribes. All we have to do is…do it.

The blessings we desire for our lives are <u>contingent on two things</u>. Do you know what they are? It's in Matthew 6:33.

1.) Seeking after God's kingdom, above everything else we seek in our lives.
2.) Seeking the right way of living that God prescribes.

If we do these two things, then, according to Jesus, all the other stuff we're continually striving after will be <u>added</u> into our lives (as God sees fit). God will <u>give</u> them to us, rather than us struggling so hard to get them.

It doesn't mean we won't work hard for what we get. It just means God is the one who's doing the *'giving'*, even as we work for it, and we're doing the *'getting'*, giving him the honor and the glory in return.

So, I guess we need to ask ourselves. Are we doing those two things? If we are, then we should start expecting. Expecting what? Expecting God to add to our lives the things we are striving for. God will come through. Why would he? Because Jesus said he would.

<u>Obey God and leave all the consequences to him.</u>

Day 92 → <u>Does God Get Tired?</u>

Here's a guarantee for us:

<u>Psalm 121: 4,5</u> → *God never rests or sleeps. <u>God is your protector</u>. He <u>watches over you</u> and <u>stands beside you</u>, lovingly sheltering you and <u>protecting you</u>.*

Do you really believe he's watching over you...and...that he's right beside you, to shelter you and protect you?

If not, then change it by making a *choice*. Make a choice with faith mixed in to remind God of what he says he'll do. Something like this: *"God your Word says you never sleep and that you lovingly watch over me to keep me safe. You promise to stand beside me, to shelter me from the storms in my life and protect me from the effects of evil. I believe you God, just help me with any unbelief I might have. You say that not one word of all of your promises have ever failed. So, I'm going to expect and wait for you to do these things.*

Remind him over and over and over again. If you're persistent, with faith mixed in, you'll see God come through on your behalf. He'll honor your faith. Why?
Because he always honors faith...100% of the time. You're going to feel his presence beside you. You're going to see his protection in the little and big things in your life. God cannot lie. He'll do what he says he'll do.

<u>**By the way**</u>: Why would God need sleep? He isn't human. He doesn't get physically tired like we do. So, if you're wondering if God's ignoring you or if he sees what you're going through, rest assured, he's not sleeping. **He notices.**

And just as that verse at the top of the page says, *'He watches over you.'* That means he's paying attention to you, to guard you. How could God do that if he weren't truly <u>noticing</u> you. God never disappoints anyone who places their trust in him.

<u>*God is never in a hurry, but God is never late.*</u>

🌳 Day 93 → <u>Can you picture yourself</u> ...

Can you picture yourself walking around weariing a helmet and a breastplate and a sword? Me neither, but don't worry, it's invisible. It's God's *spiritual* armor, and that's what we're supposed to wear if we don't want to be spiritually defeated.

Most importantly make sure you carry the '<u>shield of faith</u>' that Paul mentions as part of that amor (See Ephesians 6:16). It's meant to shield you from the arrows of your enemy.

But how often do we forget about our shield and leave it in the closet? We then get pierced with one of those arrows, and now we're wounded and out of the fight, and guess what? We can't be victorious in our troubles when that happens.

In the middle of trouble, how exactly are we supposed to use the shield of faith? Take a look at the verse below:

<u>Ephesians 6:16</u>→ *<u>Pick up</u> the shield of faith. <u>Hold it up</u> so you can stop the <u>flaming arrows</u> of the Evil One.*

The shield of faith only works when we <u>pick it up</u> and <u>hold it up</u>. What are we holding it up for? To shield ourselves from <u>the flaming arrows</u> the enemy is firing at us.

And notice they're not just arrows which can wound you...no, they're flaming arrows. They can wound you and light your whole life on fire.

Remember what Jesus told us? → **The enemy has these three goals in mind:**
1) to steal from you (things like happiness, peace, security etc.),
2) to destroy and ruin your life
3) to make you sick, and if possible, kill you.

Let's not even give him the chance.

Don't be scared when the devil attacks you. Be scared when he leaves you alone.

Day 94 → Give and Get...Take The Bet

Look at this guarantee:
Luke 6:38 Jesus speaking → *If you give to others generously, then generous gifts will be given back to you (you will be given much in return). In fact, you will be given so much in return that you won't be able to hold onto it and it will spill over into your lap, so to speak. The way that you give to others is exactly the way God will give to you.*

This is a huge promise!
The question is...what are we going to do with it? Are we going to place our bets on this promise and **ABC(D)** it? →
Agree with God that we will give generously to others,
Believe it in our hearts that he will generously give back to us.
Confess it with faith, with true confidence that it will happen.

What's the "D" for? → **D**o what he tells us to do. Start giving more. Be more generous...not just to get a lot back, but out of gratitude for all that God's given us. Then watch what happens. It may be immediate, or it may be a month, or even a year. Just watch and expect. We should expect God to honor his Word and generously give back to us so much in return that it will spill over.

Why would Jesus say something like that unless he meant it? And if he meant it, then we should believe it. We should expect to see God generously giving back to us...so much so we can't even hold onto to it. It will spill over into our laps, so to speak.

Just don't forget the very last sentence in that promise→ '*The way that you give to others is exactly the way God will give to you.*'

That can be exciting or troubling, because if we're not giving generously, we're not going to be getting much back from God. But if we give to others generously, God guarantees to give back to us more than enough. It will spill over. Our cup runneth over.

So, take the bet and give generously.

Happiness doesn't come from what we get, but from what we give.

🌳 Day 95 → **Contingencies Anyone?**

Many people don't know that God often has contingencies to his blessings. But these contingencies are not meant to restrict us from his blessings, they're meant to protect us from missing out on all those wonderful things he wants to give us.

Just to give you an example, here's a contingency worth noting→ Do you know **the first key** to opening the door to God's storehouse of blessings and prosperity?
It's seeking him first; above all the other interests we have in life.

Here is the guarantee:

Matthew 6:33 Jesus speaking→ *Seek God's kingdom above everything else in your life* (his lordship, his wisdom, his way of doing things, his realm of blessings etc.) *and seek the right way of living that he prescribes, and all the other things that you're striving for and are so concerned about, will be added to your life* (as God sees fit).

So, that's the 1st key → Seek his Kingdom first.

The 2nd key that opens the door of God's storehouse of blessings and prosperity is found in the second half of that verse above.→ Seeking the right way to live, as God prescribes. Well, how do we know what he prescribes? Luckily, God's done the homework for us. All we have to do is open his Book and apply what we read.

It's amazing to think about all the self-help books out there and all the advice on the internet people seek to meet their needs and fulfill their yearnings. Yet Jesus sums it all up with two simple keys.

So, go ahead and use those keys to open his doors to good things, and then watch how all the other things you've been striving for and concerned about will be added to your life (as God sees fit).

We can seek God with our intellect, but we can only find him with our heart.
Seeking his Kingdom involves the heart.

🌳 Day 96 → <u>Is It This Path or That Path?</u>

Take a look at these two verses:
<u>Poverbs 3:5&6</u> → *Put your trust in God with all your heart. Don't just rely only on your own understanding or your own judgment in each situation. In everything you do in your life. acknowledge him* (invite him into the middle of your situation and declare his sovereignty over your life). *Do this and he will direct your steps and show you which path to take. Plus, he'll level out the obstacles that block your way.*

Here are <u>three things</u> we can add to our plan for success and prosperity as we travel through life:
1) Put your trust in God's wisdom and direction (not looking elsewhere)
2) Don't just trust your own judgment in the situations you're in.
3) Acknowledge God, bringing him into the middle of each situation.

If we do those three things, we can claim his <u>guidance</u> on our path to success, and the removal of the <u>obstacles</u> that can make the journey so much harder. That's what we all want, right?

Who wouldn't want the creator of the universe directing their path to success and prosperity? That's what God says he will do. It's like having the most expensive success guru as your personal business and wealth consultant.

And who wouldn't want their paths to be leveled out instead of packed with hindrances? In the Hebrew, the meaning of the phrase, *'he will direct your steps'* also means he will level out the rough road and remove the obstacles that block the way.

What more could we ask for. His paths always lead to good things. So, if God is directing our steps, he'll be directing them along his paths not the world's. It only seems natural, therefore, that God would remove the obstacles and smooth out the road along the way.
That's what we have to believe God for, don't we. It makes the journey so much easier.

<u>The will of God won't take you where the grace of God can't keep you.</u>

🌳 Day 97 → Another ROADBLOCK

Isaiah 48:18 God speaking→ *Oh, if you had only paid attention to my instructions and continually obeyed them like I told you to, then you would have had peace flowing like a river….*

Who doesn't want *peace* just flowing like a river through their lives, right?

But, what did the people in this verse fail to do that kept that peace from flowing? → They weren't paying attention to God, nor were they careful to follow his instructions, and as a consequence they lost the peace. That's a roadblock to peace.

Just Reverse It → If you reverse the meaning of that verse, it becomes a promise you can cling to:
1.) **If** we pay attention to what God tells us to do.

2.) **If** we're careful to apply it to our life, and practice it over and over again until it becomes an every day part of our lives.

3.) **Then** we'll enjoy peace flowing like a river through our hearts and our lives, just as God promises.

Here's where the letters **RAP** come in.→ **R**ead it. **A**pply it. **P**ractice it over and over again. Be a 'rapper'. (What! Too cheesy for you?)☺

You know what? Medical science tells us that our bodies were designed to operate in peace. That's the way God made us. When God created the first two human beings, they lived in peaceful surroundings. They were innocent and at peace. They knew no guilt. There are plenty of studies that show that a lack of peace and feelings of guilt both have detrimental effects on the body, leading to a myriad of diseases.

Isaiah 26:3 says → God will continually keep in complete and total peace all those who let their trust be solely in him.

You see, that's what God's will is for us…to live continually in complete peace.

When we put our problems in God's hands, he puts his peace in our hearts.

Day 98 → Give and Take

Take a look at this guarantee:

Psalm 55:22 → *Give to God* (meaning, release into his hands and let go of) *all your worries and burdens* (those things that weigh you down). *If you do this, he will take good care of you* (meaning, he'll hold you up, sustain you, so you'll make it through). *In fact, he will never allow his righteous ones to be shaken* (to slip or fall flat on their faces).

You know what? God won't take our worry away for us. We have to *give* it to him. Faith is putting all our eggs in God's basket. That means our basket of worries should be empty.

I'll tell you what often happens. Believe me, I know this from my own struggles in learning this principle. We might wake up the next morning feeling pretty tired and worn-out. Why is that?
It's because we really haven't *totally* given our worries to God. We may think we've given *all of them* to him...but we really haven't. We've taken some of them back again.

You know what? God totally understands us because he made us. He smiles at us. He doesn't frown with disapproval, or lose his patience with us, or get upset with us because we keep taking our worries back. He wants us to be free of stress. He doesn't want us to carry those burdens all by ourselves. He comes along-side us, smiling, and holds out his hands, just waiting for us to give those worries back to him.

So, when the enemy starts to plant those thoughts of worry in your head, just tell him to back off and go talk to God...he's the one holding your worries, not you.

Jesus marveled at those around him, saying, *"Why do you have so little faith?"* In other words, he was sort of saying, *"Why do you worry so much?"* In a way when we worry, it shows we are lacking faith that God can come through in our situation. Let's not do that.

The lack of faith is not doubt, it is certainty.   A. Vanburen

Day 99 → Tuckered Out and Drained

It's hard to put the effort out to follow God when we feel tired and worn out, isn't it? God understands and he feels what we feel. He says he'll empower us during those times.

Here is a wonderful guarantee:

Isaiah 40:29 → *God gives strength to those who feel tired and worn out. And he gives power to those who feel powerless.*

How does God know when we need strength? Is it only when we tell him? Or, could it be he also has his eyes straight on us and is intimately aware of the details of our lives...what we're feeling and how we're faring.

And what are you going to do with that promise, anyway? Are you going to believe that God will strengthen you? Are you going to expect it? This is a perfect promise to do some verbal reminding ...to ourselves and to God.

God wants us weak!

2 Corinthians 12:9 → *My grace is all you need. In fact, my power always works best in a person's weakness.*

Some of us might be thinking, "*Wait a second! I thought God wanted us strong. Now you're saying he wants us weak? Why?*"

Well, when we finally *stop* trying to fix things in our own power and get out of the way so that God can strengthen us with *his* power, to do it his way, then we make way for a supernatural outcome.

Think about that for a second → If God's power were being displayed in our weakest moments, what might that look like? Shouldn't it look supernatural? I mean, if God's power is supernatural, then we should see a supernatural outcome, right?

There's nothing wrong with being weak, as long as God is supernaturally strong in us.

Day 100 → <u>Give Me A Plan, Will You</u>?

Here's what you need to do to become a wise and fruitful person in life, who's success and prosperity are a testimony of God's goodness in your life.

12 things to add to your plan to do well in life:

1) Get comfortable with the idea that God is excited to prosper you and give you success in life.
2) Seek his kingdom above everything else in your life, and all the other stuff you're striving for will be provided by God himself as he sees fit.
3) Seek to consistently live your life the way God prescribes.
4) Take pleasure in being in God's company and he will align your desires with his.
5) Look into God's Word deeply and carefully. Ponder it frequently, and then do what it says.
6) Use God's Word as a flashlight and spotlight to keep you from stumbling and to guide you along the path you're on.
7) Put your trust in God's wisdom and direction. Don't just trust your own judgment. Acknowledge God and invite him into the middle of each situation.
8) Don't forget that it's God who causes you to prosper, succeed and do well in life.
9) Be humble about your blessings, prosperity, and success.
10) Be careful to live with deep respect and reverence toward God.
11) Be generous and share with others the blessings God's given you.
12) Store up for yourself heavenly treasures. Make sure it's gold and silver and *not* wood, hay, or dust.

> None of these things are hard to do. They all lead to a glorious outcome in life.

<u>Just Remember</u> → God makes his way of living easy...It's us who make it hard. So, let's not do that.

Success is not measured by what you do compared to what others do. It is measured by what you do with the ability God gave you. Zig Ziegler

🌳 Day 101 → Are Your Words Full Of Faith?

Hebrews 11:1 → *Faith is believing in the reality of that which we <u>don't</u> see. It's the evidence of that which we desire and hope for.*

When we speak the promises of God, with faith mixed in, we're trusting that the reality of those words that originated in the spiritual realm will become reality for us in this earthly realm, even if we don't see it yet.

Everything God spoke originated in the spiritual realm, yet became real in the earthly realm. Think about it, when God spoke the words, *"Let there be light.",* he spoke it in the heavenly realm first and it instantly became reality in this earthly realm.

What makes God's promises become a reality in our personal lives is *faith*. It's the catalyst for turning a spiritual reality into an earthly reality. God already spoke the promises. They exist in the heavenly realm. They never fade away or become old. It's when we believe in what he already spoke in the heavenly realm that allows it to become a reality in our lives in this earthly realm.

Faith makes things possible, not easy. That's what *believing* is all about. It's putting our faith into action.

And remember this: God wants our words to <u>agree</u> with his words. Speaking words of doubt disagrees with God's words. Don't let that happen. After all, the source of faith <u>*is*</u> the Word of God.

Let's make our words agree with what God says….not just for a few hours or a few days, but all the time.

Matthew 4:4 Jesus speaking → *People don't live just by eating food alone, but they definitely live by every word that God says.*

Let's live our lives according to what God says.
The easiest way to begin is by agreeing with what he tells us.
And his promises are a great place to start.

<u>Have faith in God. God has faith in you.</u>

🌳 Day 102 → Can You Turn On The Light Please?

Take a look at this guarantee:

Psalm 119:130 → *God's Word gives light so that even those who lack direction and understanding are given insight and are made wise.*

And check this verse out:

Psalm 119:105 → *Your Word, God, is a flashlight for my feet (to keep me from stumbling) and a spotlight to my path (so I know where I'm heading).*

There are 3 things God promises us in those two verses:
1) If we use his Word for guidance, we'll be given insight that will help us act wisely.
2) Applying his Word in our lives will keep our feet from stumbling.
3) His Word will show us the right path to travel on.

Think about this→ Have you ever been in a room that's completely dark, and you tried to make your way around, only to stumble and bump into things? That's kind of what it's like when we don't have God's guidance in our lives.

What's interesting to me is that a single little match can light up an entire room. Do you think it's a coincidence that light always dispels darkness, but darkness can never dispel light? I think it's a spiritual and physical principle that God made unchangeable. The enemy of our souls can never dispel God's light with his darkness. He will always flee from it. So, we need to keep as much of that light shining in our lives as possible.

You know what I say? Don't waste time trying to stumble your way through the darkness. Use God's guidance as you travel through life. Use the light of his Word to find your way. It'll drive out that darkness, save you time, and keep you from making missteps.

Don't let your circumstances speak louder than God's Word.

God gives us opportunities to see in the dark, but it's up to us to find the light.

DAY 103 → Hire God As Your Guide. His Rates Are Low

Take a look at these 3 promises as they pertain to guidance:

Psalm 48:14 → *God, is our God forever, and he will lead and guide us all the way through our lives until the very end.*

Psalm 73:24 → *God, you are guiding me with your wise counsel and advice and it will lead me to a wonderful outcome.*

Psalm 18:36 → *God, you've cleared the path for my feet so that my feet will not stumble.*

These three verses contain simple but profound declarations on how God will guide us:

1) God will guide us all the way through our lives, **if** we let him. We're talking about the creator of the universe being our guide. Why would we look anywhere else for guidance?

2) His wisdom and advice and counsel will guide us to a glorious outcome.

3) He's cleared out all the obstacles, the rocks, roots, and ruts that could trip us up and make us fall on the path we're traveling on.

What does it feel like when God's guiding us?
I would say somehow we know it's him and not us. Little things and big things happen that feel like a God-produced serendipity.

But, here's the real question → What will make these verses come true in our own lives? Will we trust what those verses say? Will we believe them and claim them as a personal reality in our lives?

I mean, if we really believe what God is saying in those verses, then we should wholeheartedly expect him to be right there with us guiding us through the big stuff and the little stuff in our lives. We should most certainly expect a glorious outcome. We should absolutely see the obstacles being cleared out.

God's paths get you where you want to go. If we simply believe, it will take a whole lot of pressure off our shoulders in terms of what steps to take next.

God is able to make the impossible possible.

Day 104 → Can I Just Have A Little Peace Please!

Read this guarantee:
Isaiah 26:3 → *God will keep in complete and total peace all those who trust him and **let** their thoughts be fixed on him* (instead of their worries, troubles, or their fears).

How do we have *'peace'* in the midst of our troubles? By continually setting him before us.

Well, how do we continually set him before us? By fixing out thoughts on him, here and there, throughout the day, feeding our faith, not our doubts. This will give us more and more confidence to trust him in the middle of the storm, and in return, God will keep us in total peace throughout the ordeal.

And think about this. For God to keep us in a state of peace, he has to come down and zero-in on us personally, taking an interest in what's going on in our life. Have you ever thought about that?

That's how much he cares about us, to take the time to keep us in a state of peace amidst our troubles. If you're ever tempted to think that God just doesn't notice you, consider that thought.

John 14:27 Jesus speaking → *I am leaving you with a gift. Peace of mind and heart. And my peace is different from the peace the world gives, so don't let your hearts even be troubled.*

Jesus had a peace that we need and he's given it to us. How do you think he was able to sleep so soundly in the middle of a raging storm that threatened to capsize the boat he and his disciples were in? He was in a state of peace because he continually trusted God and kept his Father in heaven in front of him.

And notice the word '***let***' in that verse at the top of the page. Jesus *let* his thoughts be on God, not the troubles around him. He also let God's peace be centered in him, not the difficulties that accosted him. We should do the same.

Once you have peace with God, you get the peace of God. Rick Warren

Day 105 → Hey...I Got A Lot On My Mind!!!

People think they have a lot to worry about in their lives, but you know what Mark Twain once said:

> "*I have known a great many troubles, but most of them never happened.*"

That leaves a whole lot of wasted time worrying, doesn't it?
So, what are we supposed to do?

Take a look at this promise:

Psalm 55:22 → *Give to God* (meaning, release into his hands and let go of) *all your worries and burdens* (those things that weigh you down). *If you do this he will take care of you* (meaning, he'll hold you up, and sustain you so you'll make it through). *In fact, he will never allow his righteous ones to be shaken* (slip or fall flat on their faces).

What does God expect you to do?

1) Let go of (completely release) your worries and burdens by putting them into God's hands and not taking them back.

2) Make sure you're one of the '*righteous ones*' mentioned in that verse. How? → By continually doing the things he tells you to do. That's what '*righteous*' means (you're consistently doing what is right).

Letting go means completely releasing our grip on our worries. If we've done that, then our hands should be *empty* and the weight on our shoulders should be *lifted,* right? I mean, we should feel light and free of our burdens.

Why does it seem so hard for us to release our worries and concerns to God? Could it be that we just don't believe he'll work it all out for our benefit? Or if we do release them into God's hands, why do we seem to repeatedly take them back again? Could it be that we don't fully trust God with them?

These are the things I struggle with...how about you?

> ***Worry about nothing. Pray about anything. Trust God with everything.***

🌳 Day 106 → Do What King U. Did

2 Chronicles 26:5 → *King Uzziah <u>continually sought God</u> during the days of the prophet Zechariah, who taught him <u>to fear the Lord</u>* (meaning - to live with deep respect and reverence toward God). *As long as Uzziah <u>sought guidance</u> from God, <u>followed</u> after him, and <u>obeyed</u> him, <u>God caused</u> him to <u>succeed</u>.*

There are 4 things that Uzziah did that stand out here:
1) He <u>sought</u> God consistently
2) He learned to live with deep <u>reverence</u> and respect toward God.
3) He <u>followed</u> God's guidance
4) He <u>did</u> what God said to do.

And, because he did those 4 things, God gave him <u>success</u>.

It's no different for us. This principle is revealed all through the Bible. God is laying out for us the contingencies for success and prosperity here. Consider them to be guarantees for our own successes in life. All we have to do is follow in the steps of King U.

So, is this a promise we can claim for ourselves? My answer is "Yes". Why? → Because it's <u>a universal truth throughout the scriptures</u> that when we seek after God (for his guidance, to know him, to learn how to do what he instructs us to do), he'll bless us and help us do well in life.

So, again, how might you declare this to God? Something like this: *"God, Uzziah was no different than me. If I continually seek you and your guidance and if I live my life with a deep reverence and respect toward you, carefully following your instructions, then I know that you'll <u>cause</u> me to succeed and do well in life. For, you said it and I know it's your desire to do so. I claim this for my life, Lord."*

Bottom-Line:
1) Seek God consistently
2) live with deep respect toward him
3) Follow his leading
4) Do what he tells you to do.

<u>Just because you found God doesn't mean you should stop seeking him.</u>

Day 107 → Lemme Give You Some O' What I Got

Take a look at this guarantee:

2 Corinthians 9:8 → *God is able and more than ready to give you abundant blessings, so that you'll always have, in all circumstances, more than enough of everything as well as plenty left over to share with others.*

When God blesses you, don't just look at them as something just for you. That's the amazing thing about God, he gives us more than enough, so we can share with others. So, remember that promise above when he blesses you. Don't just receive the blessing and leave it at that. No, look around for someone to share some of it with.

- If you're financially blessed by God, share some it.
- If you're blessed with more than enough to buy groceries, think about sharing some of them.
- If you've been blessed with healing, share some comfort that God showed you with someone else.

You get the idea, right? → If God has been generous with us, then we shouldn't be stingy in any way….so give some of it away.

And notice that in that verse is the promise that God is *able and ready* to give you abundant blessings. Well, if he's able and ready to do that, then why doesn't he automatically do it? It's because he's waiting for us to do something. What is that something?

- He's waiting for us to have a giving attitude.
- He's waiting for us to have the faith to believe he'll give us more than enough so we can share it with others.
- He's waiting for us to start giving, even if he hasn't supplied us with the abundance yet.

You know what I think? It should be exciting to be generous. Not just because God's going to bless us, but because God is letting us be a little part of him. After all, who doesn't feel good when they're being generous to others?

You don't have to be rich to be generous. You have to be generous to be generous.   J. Hunt

Day 108 → What's On Your Mind?

Psalm 16:8 → *Because I continually set God before me, I know with certainty that he is close by my side. And <u>because I know</u> he's right beside me, <u>I will not be shaken</u> or defeated when trouble comes.*

That's one confident statement, isn't it?
Would you like that kind of confidence when trouble comes?

Here's the thing → None of us would probably admit it, but sometimes we act like God's not even there beside us. It;s as if he's not even there at all. In the midst of our troubles, we might tell others with our mouths, "*I know God's with me.*" but we don't say it with our actions. It's almost the opposite. We talk about our troubles a little here, a little there, thinking it won't matter. It's as if our actions are saying, "*God's not really there beside me*".

Or maybe inwardly, we're sulking or upset with God that he's allowing us to go through this trouble, especially when we feel we've been faithful. Our friends have great lives…so why us?

Wanna know how I know this? Because I speak from experience.

But why was the writer of that verse so <u>confident</u> that God was right there beside him? It's because he <u>continually</u> put God in front of him, in the forefront of his thoughts and actions…no matter what the circumstances were. He was feeding his faith and starving his doubt. So, even in the middle of trouble, he was unbendable and unshakable.

All we have to do is follow his example, right?
But how would we personally put God continually in front us? Would we read his Word and copy and paste it into our phones or onto a post-it note? Would we pray short prayers here and there throughout the day? Would we practice mindfulness?

The point I'm making is we all need to make our faith practical by applying it to our lives with concrete actions. How we do that is up to us…as long as we do it. Wouldn't you agree?

Put God before you and you will never be last.

Day 109 → <u>God Just Doesn't Listen To Me.</u>

He's listening. He says he's <u>always</u> ready to help you. *Always* means…always. How can he always be ready to help us if he's not paying attention to us? So, yes, he's listening. Do we believe it? That's the question.

Some of us might be thinking, *"I don't feel he hears me and I definitely don't see him helping me."*

Well, it could be a 'waiting' thing. Or it could be that he *is* answering you and you're just not seeing it. Or it could be something that needs changing in your life.

I think we need to do a heart-check several times a week, just to see if we're missing anything God wants to change in us?

Wanna know how to do a heart-check? Simply pray the verse below with sincerity and watch what happens.

<u>Psalm 139:23,24</u> → *Search me, God, to know what's in my heart. Examine me, to know what my thoughts are. Point out to me anything that may offend you, that you may want to change in me, and then lead me along the godly path of everlasting life.*

Beware. Do you think if you prayed that verse to God he would answer you? I do. How do I know? Because I pray it a lot and God always seems to come through to show me just *how much* he wants to change in me. Ouch!

You should try it. But don't forget I warned you. You may not like what you see, but that's ok. It's what the Bible calls *'the sanctification process'*. It's God showing us the crummy thinking, attitudes, and behavior that he wants to change in us, so we'll become more like his Son.

I can tell you from experience that it's kind of embarrassing, especially when we think we've got our Christian act together. It's amazing what God sees that we don't.

The Lord searches the heart and understands every motive behind our thoughts.

🌳 Day 110 → Want Some Wisdom?

Check out this guarantee:

Ecclesiastes 2:26 → *When people please God by doing what he tells them to do, he will give them wisdom, understanding, and joy.*

That's a good promise to grab onto. Please God by doing what he says, and he'll give you wisdom and understanding of the things of God. Not only that but we'll also have joy. Why is that? Because we were designed and built to follow God's ways. So, naturally, if we do that, it will give us a sense of fulfillment and joy.

And look at this promise:

Psalm 19: 7&8 → *God's instructions can be trusted. They make foolish people wise. God's instructions are correct for your life and bring joy to the heart.*

You know what that's saying? → If you've made foolish mistakes in your life, you don't have to anymore. Just follow his instructions and you'll gain wisdom. You'll be wise...not foolish.

> There is an old saying: ***God speaks but wisdom listens.***

And *if* you apply that wisdom to your life, then chances are you'll be making far less mistakes and that should make you happier (*joyful*).

Kind of weird, isn't it? It seems so simple to have wisdom, peace and joy...but somehow, we make it hard.
We make it hard on ourselves when we allow joy to be stolen from us. The only thing that can really steal our joy from us is sin. That's right...the **"S"** word.
I don't know about you, but I don't feel very happy or joyful when I've done what I know is wrong in God's eyes.

It's been said: "Forbidden fruit creates many jams." So, when we commit the **'S'** word, we're messin' with his blessin'! **Don't eat the forbidden fruit.**

> ***A sin does not define you, what you do next does.***

Day 111 → <u>Hey God...Can I Come In?</u>

<mark>Hebrew 4:16</mark> → *Let's approach the very <u>throne</u> of God with confidence. There we'll receive <u>his favor,</u> and <u>his goodwill,</u> and <u>his kindness</u> to <u>help</u> us in our time of need.*

Did you know that one of the privileges we have as God's children is to be able come right into God's throne-room <u>anytime</u> we want help. That's amazing when you think about it. We can walk right up to the throne of the creator of the universe and get his help, and we can be sure of a happy welcome.

Here's the thing, though. Even though that's exactly what that verse above says, many of us struggle to believe it, and I certainly can understand why. After all, God can often seem far away at times. It's pretty hard to imagine just walking up to his throne. But, the irony is, if we don't believe it, then we flat-out rob ourselves of an amazing promise of help.

People think such a thought is sacrilegious - "*I can't just walk right through the gates of heaven and right up to the throne of God. That's just not right!*" And so, they stand outside the gates wishing God would notice them.

The thing they have to grasp is: He invites us in (see Hebrews 10:19). The curtain that once separated God from humanity has been torn from top to bottom. God made himself accessible to us (see Mathew 27:51).

So, if we're his adopted, forgiven children, and we've been invited into his presence, then what are we waiting for? All we need is faith to <u>approach</u> him with confidence just as that verse above says. (Also see Ephesians 3:12).

The only reason we can come into God's holy presence at all is because the blood of Jesus cleansed us, and we are pure and without a single fault. Before Jesus, sinful humans would die if they came near God's very presence. Now we can live *with* him <u>forever</u>. I hope we never take that thought for granted. How about you?

<u>When we enter his presence with praise, He enters our circumstances with Power.</u>

Day 112 → I Don't Think God Cares About My Life

Luke 12:7 Jesus speaking → *Listen, God even knows the number of hairs on your head. So, <u>don't let</u> yourself be worried or afraid. You are more valuable to God than anything else in all his creation.*

Do you feel that God doesn't seem to care about what's going on in your life?

Then just review that promise above. God wants you to understand that if he knows the ever-changing numbers of hairs on your head, then he's also paying attention to the bigger things in your life as well…like your problems.

If you don't believe this, then it will be really hard to trust him with your worries, right?.

And, remember, Jesus is giving us a <u>promise</u>. Notice 3 things:

1) God promises to notice all the details of our lives, from the number of hairs all the way up to the bigger, more important stuff.

2) God promises he considers us more valuable than anything else in the universe…let me say it again – more than anything else in the whole universe. So, take a chance and believe that he notices you and all the details of what's going on in your life. Just make sure you invite him into the middle of your circumstances. If you keep him at a distance…then that's what you'll get.

3) We have to <u>refuse to allow</u> ourselves to worry or be afraid. How do we do that? Well, one way is to ponder the words in that verse we just covered.

Ok, I have to admit, it does seem a bit hard to believe that God actually knows the number of hairs on our heads at any given time. But, wait – if he's capable of creating millions of galaxies so big and suns so much larger than our own that we can't even wrap our heads around it, then I'm guessing that knowing how many hairs we own on our head is pretty easy for him. Wouldn't you agree?
 No matter what anyone thinks of us, God knows our heart and that's all that matters.

God knows.

🌳 Day 113 → Seeking strength from God <u>isn't a hail-Mary pass</u> at the last minute because we're in a bind.

Seeking God's strength is intertwined with a continual search to know God.
Think about that. The more we get to know God, the more we'll trust him, and that opens the floodgates for his strength to become our strength.

If God is a stranger to us, just some entity we pray to only when we need help, then our faith will be weak, and it will hinder God's strength from flowing through us. He needs to be up-close and real to us. That will only happen if we seek him diligently, carefully, and consistently.

Take a look at this verse below:

<u>Ephesians 6:10</u> → *Be strong in the Lord* (meaning - receive strength from him, live by his strength, make his strength your strength) *and be empowered with <u>his</u> power.*

God wants to give us *his* <u>personal</u> strength. He makes that clear over and over again.

Either we're receiving strength from God or we're managing the situations in our lives in our own strength. Either we get up each morning and live out the day empowered by God, or we don't.

Which is it for you? That verse above is telling us where to go for strength and if we go to God for it, we'll be empowered with his own personal strength above and beyond our own.

The only thing that could get in the way of that happening is unwillingness and lack of faith…or…throwing a hail-Mary pass at God. I think we all do that sometimes. We're super busy with our lives and we haven't been putting in the time or effort in seeking the Lord. Now trouble rears its ugly head, and we start scrambling with our prayers, throwing whatever we can at God, hoping something will stick. I'm sure you would agree that's not living in the strength of God. So, let's avoid those hail-Mary passes and '*be strong in the Lord'.*
    <u>Giving up is not an option when God made you a conqueror.</u>

Day 114 → WHAT???

Joy can be described as a calm inner gladness and contentment. I like that description...short but sweet.

But here's the thing about joy...it involves a choice.

<u>James 1:2</u> → *When you run into a lot of problems, or encounter a bunch of trials or adversities, <u>consider it</u> a <u>joy</u>.*

WHAT???? Yup...think of it as an opportunity to have joy. **How's that even possible?** The answer is in **verse 3**.→ '*Because you know that those trials are going to challenge and grow your faith. And when you make it through all that trouble, still holding tightly to your faith, you'll be even stronger when more trials come down the road.*'

Did you notice the two words – ***"consider it"***? → That's the <u>choice</u> we have to make. How are we going to *consider* the situation we're in? Are we going to look at our crummy circumstances as a chance to have joy and grow from it...or...are we going to complain and be inwardly angry at God for letting that stuff happen to us?

The choice is ours to make. Just don't leave it on the table. Make the choice. If we don't make a choice and trouble shows up, we're going to get clobbered. We may even feel defeated and dejected over our circumstances.

But what if we made a choice to consider our troubles differently, to be truly glad that it's giving us the opportunity to grow and mature from them. What if we did that?

One option is easier, and the other option is harder, but when you think about it, which is more *rewarding* – inwardly grumbling about our difficulties, or being content and even grateful for them? We can be thankful for the troubles we have, and we can be thankful for the troubles we don't have.

<u>Remember to forget the day's troubles and remember the day's blessings.</u>

Day 115 → Good Ole Abe

You know what I think we need to do?
We need to follow the example of Abraham in the Old Testament. God made a bunch of promises to him that seemed impossible for them to actually come true. But this is what Abraham did with those promises:

Romans 4:17 → *Abraham was an example to us. He <u>believed</u> that God could bring the dead back to life and that God could <u>call into existence those things that aren't even a reality yet</u>.*

Now that's faith in action! And that's what we need to do when we're in the middle of trouble, or worry, or some other struggle...<u>believing that God can call into existence that which is not real yet</u>.

That verse above says Abraham was an example for us to copy. That word '*copy*' means we can do the same thing Abraham did.

Take a look at these 3 verses:

Luke 1:37 → With God nothing is impossible.

Mathew 19:26 → With man it's impossible, but with God everything is possible.

Genesis 18:14 → Is anything too difficult for the Lord to accomplish?

Yeah, I would say God can call into existence that which isn't real yet anytime he wants. Again, it all centers around whether or not we're going to believe those verses.

In fact, it really comes down to what's filling our hearts. Is there <u>faith or doubt</u> down in there? The results depend on it, wouldn't you agree?

<u>Those who leave everything in God's hand will eventually see God's hand in EVERYTHING.</u>

Day 116 → Spiritual Blessings Anyone?

Eph 1:3 → *God has blessed us with each and every spiritual blessing that comes **from him**, from his heavenly realm, all because we are united with Christ Jesus.*

The Greek meaning of the word '*spiritual*' is '*supernatural*'.

What kind of supernatural blessings is God talking about?

- *Supernatural **Strength*** → *"I can handle anything life throws at me, by relying on Christ who gives me his supernatural strength."* (Phil 4:13)

- *Supernatural **Peace*** → *The Lord Of Peace himself will give you his peace at all times and in every situation.* (2 Thessalonians 3:16)

- *Supernatural **Hope*** → *May, God, the source of hope fill you with joy and peace because you put your trust in him, so that you will spill over with hope through his Spirit.* (Rom 14:17)
  You get the idea....God gives us his personal stuff so we can thrive, not just survive, as we live our lives with him on this earth.

And you know what? If we walk around filled with God's own stuff inside us (like his strength, his peace, his hope, etc.) we're most likely going to have a lot of joy a and a lot of peace as a result.

How do we get those spiritual blessings from God? Well, just as it says in that verse above, God has already blessed us with those gifts. All we have to do is receive them by faith.

I think a lot of God's people ask him for stuff he's already given them. They ask for strength, but God already says he's given us strength. He tells us to be strong in Him. They ask for his peace, yet Jesus already told us he's given us his peace. They ask him for hope, when God already says he's given us hope. You know what I think? We need to stop asking and start using what God's already given us.

God doesn't give us what we can handle, God helps us handle what we've already been given.

🌳 Day 117 → <u>There's something I need to mention:</u>

Many times trouble and hardships come our way because of <u>wrong choices we make</u> in our lives.

Maybe you've heard the phrase: "*We are where we are in our lives today because of the choices we've made in the past.*"

This is where it gets tricky. → Did we bring on the trouble we're encountering?...or did evil spiritual forces?...or did God?

Many people say, "*Why did God let this happen to me?*"
They often assume that when bad things happen to them that God must have caused it. After all, if he's in control and his will's always done, then he must have caused it, right?

The thing is, God doesn't always get to have his way in our lives. Why? Because we often won't let him. He won't force us to go his way. He'll do everything he can to reach out to us, but if we aren't listening, or we ignore his nudges, then he'll just let us go our own way, even if it's going to lead us smack dab into trouble.

God is not going to force his people to take part in his plan to bless them. So, if we move out of God's plan of blessings and protection, then we'll just be more vulnerable to trouble coming our way.

Now I know you and I are in good standing with God, but there might be times when we jump the gun on God and kind of do what we think is best instead of what he thinks is best. That usually happens when we don't have our spiritual hearing-aids in, or we're just plain disregarding his prodding. The good news is that God allows U-turns and that's all we have to do - turn and go God's way.

James 4:7 tells us to '*Submit ourselves to God.*' We all know that verse. But it's the verse before it that explains why. Verse 6 says, God sets himself against the proud, but gives favor to the humble. You see, it's not being humble that keeps us from submitting to God's instructions. That's how we get *ourselves* into trouble, right?

<u>To walk out of God's will is to step into nowhere</u>

🌳 Day 118 → Can You Trust God?

Ernest Hemingway once said: *"The best way to find out if you can trust somebody is to…trust 'em."*

You know what? We can apply that to trusting God as well. Just go all in and try it. It's the best way to find out if you can trust him. There's nothing to lose but *doubt* itself.

With that in mind, look at this guarantee below:
<u>Romans 15:13</u> → *God, the true source of **hope** itself, will <u>fill</u> you* (Greek meaning – fill you completely, to the brim) *with <u>joy</u> and <u>peace</u>, because you **let** your <u>trust</u> be in him* (not in anything else). *If you do this, <u>then</u> you will <u>overflow</u> with confident hope through the power of the Holy Spirit.*

Notice where the <u>peace</u> is coming from → God, no other source but God. Not YouTube, social media, counselors, you name it.

Notice what he'll do with that peace → He'll fill us up to the <u>brim</u> with it. That means there's no more room for anything else like worry, troubled thoughts, anxiousness, or fear.

Notice what we have to do → *<u>trust</u>* him…really and truly trust him. No doubts, no wavering, just total confidence in his wisdom, his ways, his timing, his goodness, and his power.

Notice that <u>joy</u> and <u>hope</u> come with it. → It's a package deal.

That word '***let***' is the key to that verse. It means '*letting*' ourselves trust God. It means *not letting* ourselves doubt. It means giving ourselves permission to have faith.

The bottom-line is this → A person who is *filled* with joy and peace and overflows with confident hope, is *not* a person who is worried or troubled or fearful. Am I right? So let's do our part, and wait expectantly for God to do his.

<u>Joy is peace dancing and peace is joy at rest.</u> F.B. Meyer

🌳 Day 119 → <u>Do You Struggle With Believing God?</u>

Some of us might be thinking, *"Well, what if I struggle believing that God promises will actually happen for me?"*

Answer→ That's ok. Struggling with the things of God helps our faith grow. Keep reminding God of what he guarantees and declare his promises throughout the day. Soon it will build into faith. It will naturally spill out of you because it's coming from the abundance of your heart.

Do you remember what Jesus said? Luke 6:45 → *Out of the abundance of what's in your heart, that's what your mouth will speak.*

When you speak God's truth you will always see results.

How do we know that? → 3 reasons:
1.) His promises always come true...whether we believe them or not. They just won't come true in our own lives unless we believe.

2.) His Word is alive and actively working in us if we allow it. If we don't, then we won't see the power of his Word in our lives.

3.) His Word never returns empty. It always accomplishes what he intended, regardless of the amount of faith we have. God speaks and it happens. Plain and simple.

<u>Here are the 3 verses that say that.</u>

2 Samuel 22:31 → *"All of God's promises come true."*

Hebrews 4:12 → *"God's word is alive and actively working in us."*

Isaiah 55:11 → *"My Word will always accomplish all I want it to. It always produces results everywhere I send it.*

Remember this → <u>Faith</u> is developed by focusing on God's truth. <u>Doubt</u> is developed by focusing on the enemy's lies. Which do you want...faith or doubt?

I knew it! I knew you'd choose faith. ☺ So, feed your faith...focus on the truth.

<u>When in doubt, don't.</u>

Day 120 → God's Pretty Clear On This

Lamentations 3:25 → *The Lord is GOOD* (Hebrew meaning→ he gives good things to help us thrive and do well in life) *to those who seek him* (diligently, carefully, and consistently, out of hunger to know him). *Consequently,* (as a result of seeking him and trusting him) *they wait for him to act* (they look to him with expectation and confidence, not looking elsewhere).

You can see that God is pretty clear on what he requires us to do in order to receive really good things from him in our lives:
         * Seek him   * Trust him   * Wait on him

Do these 3 things in all their fullness and you can expect God to give you good things to help you thrive and do well in life. How can we be certain of that? Because God never lies. That means that verse at the top of the page is totally true...not partly true, completely true. All that's missing is our faith.

How do we learn to *have faith*? By seeking to know him out of a hunger to experience him. If we're not hungry for God, we probably won't seek to know him. And if we don't know him very well, we probably won't put our faith in him that much.

The only way we're going to truly trust God with what he says is to seek him to know him intimately.

How do we *seek* him?
* **Diligently** = to apply effort, to work at it with attention and persistence, not haphazardly, not with casuality.

* **Consistently** = not sporadically, but regularly, in an organized fashion using fortitude and discipline.

* **Carefully** = the word *carefully* means full-of-care. It doesn't mean to randomly open your Bible and point your finger to any verse and it doesn't mean turn on YouTube and watch any sermon that just shows up (although I do believe God can use those methods to reach us). It means to put some thought into it, to use some care.

Once you have tasted the goodness of God, nothing else will satisfy.

Day 121 → Where Does Your Peace Come From?

All of us want peace in our lives, would you agree?
But the question is how do we get it and what does God promise about it?

Perhaps it would be good to explain what the word *'peace'* means. So, here's a good definition derived from the Greek meaning of the word → *It's the freedom from all worries, freedom from being troubled, freedom from anxieties and fears, freedom from being agitated over things, freedom from inner and outer conflicts.*

That pretty much sums it up for me, but when you add it to the Old Testament Hebrew meaning for *'peace'* which is the word "*shalom*" it kind of rounds it out even more: shalom peace is *quietness, tranquility, safety, contentment, health, prosperity, with no worries or fears*. **Mix those definitions together** and you have an amazing reason to want peace in your life. I mean, who wouldn't want all those good things, right?

So, you wanna know how to get peace? Read this verse below:

Romans 8:6 → *If we set our minds on just satisfying the needs and desires of our 'flesh', it will lead to a spiritually dead life, but if we set our minds on the Holy Spirit, it will lead to life and peace.*

If we want peace in our lives, then it really comes down to what we set our minds on. If we're living just to satisfy our '*self*', irrespective of what God wants, then that's what we've set our minds on. Even though it seems like we're having fun doing our own thing, deep down inside we'll be void of peace. Imagine inviting Jesus to go along with us as we live that lifestyle. Would he feel at peace?

But it's simple enough to flip the switch. We can set our minds on God instead. It's just a choice we make. And as we continue to practice spending time with God, we'll draw closer to him instead of the world. We'll feel his peace as we do so, because in God's presence is peace in all of its fullness.

> *"Peace doesn't come from finding a lake with no storms. It comes from having Jesus in the boat."* J. Ortberg

🌳 Day 122 → You Got Enough?

2 Corinthians 9:8 → *God is happy to give you <u>more than you need</u>, so you'll have plenty of everything you need and <u>enough left over to share with others</u>.*

How is this a promise you can claim? → *"God, you say that you're happy to give me more than I need, with enough left over so I can share with others. I would love to see you do that. I'm receiving this promise from you and I will live up to my end of the blessing. I will be generous and share with others."*

Anne Frank once wrote: *"No one has ever become poor by giving."* How true that is, wouldn't you agree?

Remember this → Whatever wealth and possessions we've accumulated in life, they're ultimately given to us by God, and they're ultimately his anyway, if he's the king of our lives, right? So, nothing we have should be held onto too tightly by us. Be generous and share it with others just like God has been generous with us.

Winston Churchill said: *"We make a living by what we get, but we make a life by what we give."*

Here is a wonderful guarantee:
Luke 6:38 Jesus speaking → *Give to others <u>generously</u> and it will be given back to you generously. You will be given <u>so much more in return</u>, that it will be poured out into your life with no space left for more. For, the amount you give to others <u>will determine</u> the measure you will receive in return.*

Give generously and get way more in return. Sounds better than a stock portfolio, doesn't it?

Just don't miss the last part of that verse. The amount you give to others will <u>determine</u> how much you will receive in return. That can be exciting, or it can make us nervous. After all, if we aren't being generous how can we expect God to be generous with us?

> *<u>Our generosity is measured not by how much we give but by how much we keep.</u>*

Day 123 → Are You Gonna Be Faithful To Me God?

<u>2 Thessalonians3:3</u>→ *God is always faithful* (meaning - he's always true to his word and always does what he says he'll do). *He will <u>strengthen</u> you and <u>protect</u> you <u>from evil</u> (or the evil one).*

Has God ever been unfaithful to you?
It's a yes or no question. If he's faithful, then he'll do what he says he'll do. It's up to us to believe that he'll strengthen us and protect us. He's willing and ready to do it. We're the apple of his eye. He wants his children strong, not weak...protected, not vulnerable to harm.

The Greek word for *'strengthen'* in that verse means to make you so strong that you're firmly fixed in place, immovable. Nothing's going to shake you. It goes hand in hand with protection from evil. You're unfaltering and unbendable.

Here's the thing we need to remember:
The battles we go through are not for us to fight alone. We must let God into the struggle. That's where our strength and protection from the evil-one comes from.

Take a look at this promise:

<u>Deuteronomy 20:4</u> → *God goes with you, <u>to fight for you</u> on your behalf and <u>he will give you the victory</u> against your enemies.*

God always wants to be right in the middle of our struggles...right smack dab in the middle. He wants us to win every single battle...every one of them. He knows that won't happen without his <u>strength</u> and <u>protection</u>.

Don't go out into the big bad world without God's strength and protection. If you do, you are setting yourself up for struggles. There are evil forces that don't like you because you're a child of God who doomed them to eternal separation from all things good. They have nothing to lose but to take you down with them. It's their way of spitting in God's eye. So, carry protection. Are you packin'?

<u>Fight all your battles on your knees and in the end you'll be standing.</u>

🌳 Day 124 → Was That You Talking To Me God?

God loves to talk to us. We just need to learn to listen to his voice. But how do we know if it's God's voice we're hearing and not just our own? Here's one way:

John 10:27 Jesus speaking → *My sheep hear my voice…*

That's how Jesus described the believer's ability to hear his voice. If they hear his voice, then two things are happening:
1) Jesus is calling out to them, just like a shepherd would his sheep.
2) The sheep are listening and recognize his voice.

How do sheep know their shepherd's voice? Because they spend a lot of time with him. That's also how we'll know if it's God's voice we're hearing. – we spend a lot of time with him.

Part of a shepherd's job is to guide his sheep to where they can drink, rest, and be safe from danger. That's just what Jesus will do for us as our Great Shepherd. But the sheep had to be willing to follow his lead. They need to trust their shepherd. So it is with us.

And don't forget that God has given us his Spirit to live inside us, to guide us and counsel us. I think many of us have never really been taught much about the Holy Spirit. He ends up being some entity in the background of our Christian lives. What a shame, don't you think? The wisdom of God is right there inside of us. All we have to do is ask the Holy Spirit to guide us.

But how can we expect him to guide us if we don't recognize his voice. I would say that the Holy Spirit speaks to us in a still small voice…whispers. And he nudges us with gentle prodding so we'll go in the direction he wants us to go. It's up to us to be able to hear his voice and feel his nudges. That means we have to make ourselves more sensitive, focused, and less distracted, so we can hear and feel His counsel. Jesus called the Holy Spirit our '*Helper*'. The Greek meaning of that word is Counselor, Advocate, and Comforter. The truthful reality is we have as much guidance from God as we want. We just have to put in our spiritual hearing aids and wear our pacemakers, so we can hear his voice and have a more sensitive heart.

God does not give guidance to those who want to run their own life.

🌳 Day 125 → I Wanna Be Just Like My Big Brother.

You know what? There is no one who can do a better job at being a father to us than our heavenly Father. He knows just how to love us and encourage us. He wants his kids to grow up and become mature just like their big brother, Jesus. That sounds kind of weird doesn't it? But Jesus was the one who called us his brothers and sisters.

Not only does God want to be a father to us, he wants to be our king. As our king, he wants us to stay within the boundaries of his kingdom, so we'll stay safe and well protected.

I think too many of us wander beyond the borders of God's kingdom into the enemy's territory and consequently get ourselves in trouble. Take a look at this verse below:

Isaiah 30:21 → *If you leave God's paths and go astray, you will hear a voice behind you saying, "No, that's the wrong path, this is the way you should go.*

Notice the voice is *behind* us, not in front of us. That's because we're on the wrong path. The real question is, do we hear his voice at all?

John 10:27 Jesus speaking → *My sheep hear my voice and they listen to me. I know them and they follow me.*

I can tell you from my own experience, as one of his sheep, I have traveled down wrong paths that only led me straight into the brambles. It was because I was deaf to that voice behind me, telling me to stop and get back on the right path. My shepherd was calling after me, but I just wasn't listening. I crossed the boundaries of his kingdom right into enemy territory. Don't make this mistake yourself.

Mark 4:24 Jesus speaking → *Be careful to pay attention and understand what you hear from me. If you do this then more understanding will be given to you.*

With all the distractions we have in life, it gets harder to hear our shepherd. But, when we're careful to pay attention to him, it makes it a whole lot easier to stay within the safety of his Kingdom.

> *<u>To hear God's voice you must turn down the world's volume.</u>*

Day 126 → Hey God, Can I Hang Out With You?

Psalm 73:28: *It feels good for me to draw closer and closer to God, to stay in his presence. I have made his presence my refuge.*

The end of that verse is important. Notice the words, *"I have made his presence my refuge."*

That's what we have to do. We have to make the choice to do that ourselves. Drawing closer to God is one thing but *making* his presence a place we '*dwell*' in during the storm we're going through, is a choice we alone have to make.

So....**MAC** it. → **M**ake **A C**hoice

Some of us might be thinking, *"When I try to get into his presence, it just doesn't work. All I feel is the worry and stress over the trouble I'm going through."*

Listen, I know exactly what that feels like. I've been there myself. But, let me ask you this → When you've drawn close to God in the past, did you feel safe in his arms? Did you feel a sense of peace and rest...instead of worry and turmoil? That's being in God's presence. That's making God your refuge. Whatever you did to experience that is what you need to do again.

How do we get into God's presence?

James 4:8 tells us that → *If we draw near to God then he will draw near to us.*

Psalm 46:10 says → *Be still and come to know that I am God..*

So, what do those two verses tell us? → That we need to quiet ourselves and focus on God, shutting out all distractions so we can draw near to God in mind and spirit.

How do we know we've been in the presence of God? → Joy, because in the presence of God is the fullness of joy.

If you think about it, there is no other place on this crazy mixed-up planet that is safer than being in God's presence.

Day 127 → Are You Really Offering Me All That?

Isaiah 41:10 → *Don't worry or be troubled or afraid about anything, for I, God, am with you* (there is no one greater in the entire universe who could be with you).
And, *don't be discouraged about the situation you're in, for I am your God* (I personally care about you, deeply. Nothing is too difficult for Me.)
If you refuse to worry or be discouraged and you put your trust in Me, I will do the following:
• *I will **strengthen** you* (meaning, I will make you stronger emotionally, physically, and spiritually)
• *And I will help you* (meaning – I will come to your aid and protect you).
• *I will hold you up with my victorious right hand* (meaning, you'll be victorious because I am always victorious... you won't fight the battle alone).

Where in that promise does it leave any room for worries, anxiety, fear, or discouragement? As far as I can see, nowhere.

I mean, here's the highest being in the universe – our own creator, offering to strengthen us and help us and give us absolute victory. Who wouldn't want that?

Here's an important question for you → What would keep you from enjoying the benefits of that promise above? Yup...not believing and receiving what God is offering to do for you. I mean if you think about it, there is just a fine thin line between receiving or not receiving those blessings. That thin line has a name – FAITH.

I find it helpful in my own life to remind God of what he said he'd do. God certainly doesn't need to be reminded, but it's more for my benefit, not God's. It helps me stay in 'faith-mode'. It feeds my faith and starves my doubt. Try it yourself. Remind him.

After reminding him, I thank him for what he's going to do for me. Then I wait with expectancy, because not only is faith believing for the impossible, it's also watching and waiting with expectancy for it to happen. It takes practice, but it's a simple formula that works for me.

__Reminding God of his promises will remind you of his promises.__

🌳 Day 128 → <u>You know what's funny?</u>

When trouble or hardships come their way, people often think, "*Why did God let this happen to me?*"
God didn't do it to them...they did it to themselves. You know what often keeps God's blessings away and trouble close at hand? If he tells us to go one way (to keep us out of trouble) and we continue to go the opposite. Things aren't going to go so well for us.
Hebrews 3:12 → *Watch out and be careful that unbelief and sin-bent thoughts don't lead you off the path of following God.*

Some of us have one foot in God's Kingdom and one foot in the world. According to the Bible, that's called divided-loyalty (See James 1) We're loyal to our life in the world and we're loyal to God. But, according to God all that does is make us waver in our commitment to him. He says we'll be doubleminded and unsettled in all our ways.
The good news is God allows U-turns. It's as simple as that. If we've been running with the world, then we just need to turn around and start running with God. But we can't run with both, because they're going in opposite directions. If we've been running with the world, then we just need to make a U-turn and step right back into running with God. That's what God calls '*repentance*'. I think we've grown to dislike that word. Repentance is only for sinners...not us.

Now, I know that neither of us are running with the world, but if you ever catch yourself doing that...just make a U-turn. There were times in my life where I would allow myself to watch tv shows that were grounded in the ways of the world, not the ways of God. However, the more I got to know God, I saw how I was being influenced by the wrong stuff. I made a U-turn and committed to keeping my mind pure. I just can't live a life of *divided loyalty* any longer. How about you?

<u>*Sin is turning from God to self.*</u>
<u>*Repentance is turning from self to God*</u>

Day 129 → I Want To Be Prosperous…

1 Chronicles 22:13 → *You will prosper and be successful if you are careful to obey all that God tells you to do in his instructions.*

God made this guarantee to Joshua, but it applies to us as well because it's universally expressed to all of God's people throughout the Bible. So, claim it for yourself! God wants you to.

And take a look at the guarantee below:

1 Kings 2:3 → *Walk through life in obedience to him, and keep all of his instructions that are written in his Book of Instructions. Do this, so that you may prosper and succeed in all you do and wherever you go.*

There it is – obedience – doing what God tells us to do. There are many verses in the scriptures that say the same thing. It's pretty simple, isn't it?

So, why do so many of us struggle with it?

I personally believe it comes down to who's sitting on the throne in our lives. Who's in charge? God or us? If it's God, then all his instructions become a lot easier to follow, and blessings and prosperity will follow. If it's us, then things get a whole lot harder.

If we want God to prosper us and if we want him to help us succeed, then we need to **MAC** it. (**M**ake **A C**hoice).
What's the choice? → Who's going to be on the throne of our lives. One way to prove that God's on the throne in our daily life is to be diligent and careful to do what he tells us to do in his Word. It's not just reading it and saying a prayer. Nope. It's doing it.

In fact, God guarantees us in **James 1:25** that if we spend the time to carefully look at his Word and not forget what it says, but in fact do what it says, then God will go out of his way to bless us. Sounds good to me. How about you?

Obedience is not a matter of earning God's love; it is a way we express our love for God.

Day 130 → <u>No Weapons Allowed</u>

<mark>Isaiah 54:17</mark> God speaking → *No weapons of any form used against you will succeed…This is one of the good things my faithful servants get. Their victory comes from me."*

What kind of weapons are we talking about?
I think it includes words people use as weapons to hurt us.
Or, ways people try to deceive or manipulate us.
Or, physical harm done to us.
And of course, the spiritual weapons of the enemy to weaken our faith, to defeat us and make us doubt God.

So, the question is: What will you do with this promise? Yeah, I know I ask that question a lot. But it's where the rubber meets the road. Is that verse at the top of the page just a bunch of words or does it have power and meaning in your life? It will only be a reality to us personally when we believe it.

I would suggest onfessing it over and over again, to feed your faith and starve your doubt. Something like this. → *"God you say no weapon used against me will succeed. That means I may get attacked, but my enemies won't succeed. I receive this truth into my life because I'm your faithful servant. You never lie. Thank you for making it true in my life."*

Just remember, as the promise above says, The victory comes from God…not through our own efforts, not from friends, or self-help books, not from therapists, or YouTube. And not from Facebook or Tik Tok. All of those things might help you…but the victory…it comes from God.

It also says in that verse above, that victory is one of the things God gives to his faithful servants. Are you one of God's faithful servants? Most of us would say *'yes'* and that's the way it should be. But if we're hiding anything from our King, then we've become unfaithful. There are many stories in the Bible where one of God's faithful servants kept secrets from the Lord. One that comes to mind is David and Bathsheba. We would do well to keep our life an open book to God. He sees our deepest secrets anyway. So, lay them out.
<u>God will protect his faithful ones.</u> 1 Samuel 2:9

Day 131 → Do You feel Your Prayers Reach Heaven?

What if I told you that your prayers don't have to rise any higher than your mouth before God hears them. That's right, the one you're praying to lives inside you...*if* you've received the gift of pardon for all the crummy stuff you've done in your life.
Take a look at these two guarantees:

2 Corinthians 6:16 (God speaking)→ "*I will live in them and I will walk with them and I will be their God and they will be my people.*"

And:

Romans 8:10→ *Christ the king lives within you, so you are made spiritually alive because God has fully accepted you as his child....*

So, the author of our faith lives within us and he's just waiting to hear our words of faith.
Too many of us don't speak our faith. Instead, we speak our doubts. "I don't feel well." "I'm not very good at that." "I'm lonely." "No one cares about me."

Why not speak what God is saying, instead. I mean, his words are the real truth, right? So, let's say what he says.

Check out what Jesus said,

John 6:63→ "*The words I speak to you are Spirit* (God-breathed) *and they are life* (meaning - they are living, alive in this world)."

Here's my point. Don't miss this → When we speak the promises of God, those words are God-breathed ...meaning, they're alive and real in this *earthly* realm, because God made them alive in the *heavenly* realm where they originated. I mean, think about it. When God spoke in the *heavenly* realm and said, "*Let there be light.*" What happened? Light became real in the *earthly* realm. God's words are a spiritual reality that become a reality on earth through our faith. We need to live in that spiritual reality just as much as we live in this earthly reality.

Human unbelief cannot alter the reality of God's words.

Day 132 → Be Absolutely Certain

Romans 8:28 → *We know* (Greek meaning - to be convinced with certainty) *that if we love God, he will cause each and every detail of our lives to work together* (blended and woven together) *so that it turns out in the end for our own good.*

Here's a question for you:
Are you convinced with absolute certainty of that promise above? Do you believe that God can take all the details of your situation and turn them into good, for your benefit? If not...then why not?
It's ok to question ourselves about these things. It's what makes our faith become real.

Sometimes I think it would be easier to just simply believe than *not* believe. The difference between the two is simply...a choice...nothing more.

By the way, you probably already know this: When it says that God will work it all out for our own good, it doesn't always mean the end-result will be what we want or expect, right?
We have to look at it through God's lens, not our own. God might have something completely different in mind for us. If we were to lose a limb in an accident, God can take what the evil-one meant for harm and turn it into good if we let him. We just have to make sure we don't stand in the way. Some of us might become angry at God if that situation happened to us. If that's the case, then we're stuck with a lemon when God was trying to make lemonade from it.

But, what we can definitely hang our hat on is this→ It will always be for our benefit...our good, because God is always good to us...all of the time.

Do you believe God is *always* good to you? Do you believe he'll blend and weave the occurrences in your life so they help you?
Let God turn your lemons into lemonade.

Day 133 → Hey, Where's Your Treasure At?

Luke 12:34 Jesus speaking→ *Where your true treasure is, that's where the desires of your heart will be also.*

I guess I should ask, what are you going to do with that verse? I suggest **MAC**'ing it.→ **M**ake **A C**hoice early on, that you'll make it your priority to focus your heart on storing up heavenly wealth – God's gold and silver.
Live for the true heavenly gold and silver. Stay away from the wood, hay and sawdust.

Art Buchwald once wrote, *"The best things in life aren't things."* How true! That's what we're talking about here, right?

Ponder the verse below:
Matthew 16:2 Jesus speaking→ *What does it benefit you if you gain all the wealth and possessions this world has to offer, but you forfeit your life in the process? After all, what is more valuable than the eternal worth of your soul?*

You already know this, but it's worth repeating: Our life is shaped by the choices we make and ultimately, it's our responsibility to make the choices we're willing to live with…for eternity.

Sometimes I think many of us don't take eternity seriously. It's so out there we just can't relate to it. But that's a big mistake, because everything we do here on earth has a bearing on how we'll spend our lives in eternity.
Which do you think will last into eternity? The gold and silver or the wood, hay, and sawdust? Which do you think will make it through God's final assessment of our lives when we finally stand before him? The wood, hay, and sawdust will be burned up. It doesn't have eternal value. It's worthless in the light of eternity and what God values in us.

The rewards God talks about giving us at his Bema Seat are based on the quality of metal…not wood.

Where is your treasure? Let's MAC it. Make A Choice to store up for ourselves God's gold and silver.

🌳 Day 134 → <u>I Want That Camping Gear!</u>

Deuteronomy 29:5 → *For 40 years I led you through the desert, and yet, through it all, your shoes and clothes never wore out. I kept you fed with supernatural food just so that you would <u>know</u> that I am your God.*

Think about this. Way back in Exodus, in the days when the Israelites were leaving Egypt to go to the Promise Land (that place that the 10 spies reported on...the land that God described as rich with abundance and was theirs for the taking, free of charge), all they had to do was trust God to lead and he would take good care of them. **It's the same for us today**. Just trust and obey and he'll lead the way.

And don't forget, that through the wilderness, he provided food and water and their clothes and shoes never wore out...for 40 years! Yeah baby...that's some durable camping gear! They don't make it like that anymore. <u>They didn't lack anything</u>...anything, in that desolate wasteland of a wilderness (see Deuteronomy 8:3,4).

That wasn't even the promised land where all the wonderful blessings were waiting that God had planned for them.

You and I go through wildernesses in our lives and God is willing and able to take very good care of us as we go through them. Am I right? So, what did God want from the Israelites back then, and what does he want from us today? → Trust....to trust him in all aspects of our journey through this life. Can we do it? I think we can.

Does God love us any less than the Israelites? If he was willing to take really good care of them and provide for their needs, then he'll do the same for you and me. The question is – do we believe it? But you know what kept the Israelites from entering God's land of plenty? It was their lack of trust because of their unbelief.

Unbelief is always at the very core of a lack of trust. So, I'll ask you again, do you really believe God will take good care of you?

<u>Talk unbelief and you will have unbelief. Talk faith and you will have faith</u>

Day 135 → You Mean I Can't Worry Anymore?

Arthur Roche once wrote: *"Worry is a thin stream of fear trickling through the mind. If allowed to continue, it cuts a deep channel into which all other thoughts are drained."*

Don't let that happen to you. Don't hold onto any of your worry. Get rid of it quickly. Just give it back to God again...and again...and again.

And just do what God tells us to do in the verse below:
Psalm 46:10 → Be still (Hebrew meaning – sink down and relax, just let it go) and *learn to know* that I am God.

That phrase *"learn to know that I am God"* in the Hebrew language means it's a *learning* process. It takes time. So, don't be hard on yourself.

LUKE 12:7 Jesus speaking → *Listen, God even knows the number of hairs on your head. So, don't let yourself be worried or afraid. You are more valuable to God than anything else in all of his creation.*

Why would God bother to count the number of hairs on your head, which is pretty insignificant if you think about it. It's because he's making a point here – You matter so much to him, that he pays attention to the little stuff as well as the big stuff going on in your life. If he didn't care, he wouldn't bother to count your hair, right?

So what are we worried about? If God is paying attention to what's going on in our lives, then what's there to worry about. He's our heavenly Father and we're his children. What does a loving father do? He lovingly guides, and lovingly provides, and lovingly protects his children. That's what he promises to do for us.

Plus, we're royalty. Just think about that for a moment. What does royalty look like in kingdoms around the world? Pretty nice huh? God expects us to behave in a way that represents his monarchy. But the perks are worth it. So, stop the worrying and live like a royal.

Worrying is like paying a debt you don't owe.

Day 136 → Want Your Prayers Answered?

John 15:7 Jesus speaking → ***If** you <u>abide</u> in me* (meaning, <u>remain</u> close to me, in a deep relationship with me) *and my words <u>remain</u> in you* (meaning, you remember them and do what they say), ***then*** *ask for anything you want and it will be given to you*.

Here are **two criteria** for our prayers to get answered:

1) <u>Abide</u> in him.
You might be wondering what that means. It simply means to remain close to him through good times and bad (staying within the sphere of his love, his care, his will, his blessings, and protection). Too often we draw near to Christ in the good times, in moments when we feel emotionally connected to him.
But when circumstances get tough, we can tend to move away from God rather than drawing closer. Don't let that happen. Just remain in him in every situation.

2) <u>His Word needs to be abiding in us</u>.
This simply means his words of instructions need to remain with us, not ignored or forgotten by us, but instead, leading us to live our daily lives in agreement with them.

Note: Notice the word '***then***' in that verse. It's an adverb. It usually indicates what comes next. <u>Example</u>→ If we are remaining close to him and his words live in us, causing us to do what he instructs us to do, *<u>then</u>* we can ask what we want from God and receive it because it will be in agreement with his will.

It might be that many of us think God should automatically answer our prayers. But that's not necessarily true. In fact, the word ***"if"*** and the word ***"then"*** in the verse above, hold the key to that happening.

There are a lot of ***"<u>if's</u>"*** and ***"<u>then's</u>"*** in the Bible and they hold the key to many of God's promises coming true in our lives.
If we do our part – the ***"if's"***, then God will do his part – the ***"then's"***. Pretty simple formula when you think about it.

<u>Mind your "P's" and "Q's" with your mother, but mind your "If's" and "then's" with your father…your father in heaven.</u>

🌳 Day 137 → <u>You Call This Thing Called 'Life' Fun?</u>

There's an old saying among the cowboys of the Old West:
"Glass half empty or glass half full. Either way you look at it, you won't be going thirsty."

That's a great way to see the situations in our life, isn't it? Whether your life is half empty or half full, either way, you won't be losing out on God's blessings.

Some of us might be asking, *"How can hardships be blessings?"*

Yeah, I get it. You know what I think it is? **Many of us don't see our lives as God sees them.** We fail to look at our circumstances through the same lens God does.

We usually see life from our own perspective, and so when bad stuff happens to us, or we don't get what we were really hoping for…well, we kind of throw a hissy fit. Come on, don't tell me you don't. We all do it. We just do it in different ways. I bet God chuckles when he sees us do it, too.

Look at how God describes his way of thinking and doing things:

<u>Isaiah 55:8</u> → *My thoughts (the way I see things) are nothing like your own thoughts (how you see things), and my way of doing things are not like your way of doing things.*

If we can start to see our circumstances (whether good or bad) the way God sees them, we'll handle life a 'whole lot better'-- pardon my grammar. ☺

So, is your glass half full or half empty? Let's strap on our monocles and start seeing our lives through God's eyes. – We're blessed.

<u>Don't let your struggles become your identity. The struggle's real, but so is our God.</u>

Day 138 → <u>Just to summarize</u>

My guess is you probably already know this. The blessings we desire for our lives are basically <u>contingent on two main things</u>. Wanna know what they are?

1.) Seeking after God's kingdom, above everything else we seek in our lives.
2.) Seeking the right way of living that God prescribes.

If we do these two things, then, according to Jesus, all the other stuff we're continually striving after will be <u>added</u> into our lives (as God sees fit). God will <u>give</u> them to us, rather than us struggling so hard to get them. It doesn't mean we won't work hard for what we get. It just means God is the one who's doing the '*giving*', even as we work for it, and we're doing the '*getting*', giving him the honor and the glory in return.

Why did God make seeking after those two things <u>the keys</u> to prospering? → Because he's wise and he knows material prosperity can hurt us if we aren't prepared to manage it well. If we have our priorities wrong or we lack self-control, we can get into a heap of trouble very quickly.
So, God made sure that the prosperity <u>that comes from him</u> can <u>only come by</u> seeking him first, <u>above</u> everything else in our lives.

When we seek God first, we get our priorities straightened out. We gain wisdom from him on how to handle the blessings he sends us. With God being first in our lives, we'll stay away from the dangers that prosperity can entrap us in.

Money and things of prosperity have a proper place in our lives, but if we *don't* do what's wise with them, they'll eventually rule over us with the potential to cause us problems.

<u>A wise person should have money in their head but not in their heart.</u>
Jonathan Swift

🌳 Day 139 → <u>Realizing & Believing</u>

<u>**Psalm 121:2,7**</u> → I <u>realized</u> that my help and my protection is <u>only</u> from God, the creator of the universe. <u>He will keep me from</u> every danger and every form of evil as he <u>watches over my life</u>.

Let me ask you a question: Is there a greater source of help and protection available to us other than the creator of the universe? **Nope**. It comes down to two things in order for this promise to work for us:
1.) <u>Realizing</u> that it's really only God who can help and protect us in our lives. We can look to other sources other than God, but ultimately it's God who determines our safety.
2.) <u>Believing</u>, really truly believing that God is watching over our lives, keeping us from danger and all types of evil.

So, it's *realizing* and *believing*.
As with any of God's promises, it's about what we're going to do with that promise? It's useless to us if we don't do something with it, wouldn't you agree? I think we should declare it to ourselves, to God, and to the enemy.

I suggest **ABC**'ing it.
Agree with what God is saying in his Word, that he will help you and protect you.
Believe the promise in your heart that he will do what he says he will do, personally in your life.
Confess it over and over again, to feed your faith and starve your doubts.

If we believe what that promise above says, then we should *expect* to be helped by God today. And we should *expect* that we will be protected by him as well. Expecting goes beyond just asking for God's help and protection.

The word '*expecting*' means to regard something as likely to happen. It's anticipating, awaiting, and looking for something to take place. So, let's *realize*…*believe*…and *expect* God to help and protect us.

<u>Expecting God to come through always should follow trusting God to come through.</u>

Day 140 → Did you know God's is looking for you?

Take look at this promise:

2 Chronicles 16:9 → *God ceaselessly searches the whole earth in order to strengthen* (Hebrew meaning– to make strong, to strongly support and to enable to prevail) *those whose hearts are fully committed to him* (Hebrew meaning– those who have given themselves completely to him, whose hearts are completely his). *He wants to strengthen them.*

How does God do that? How does he search the whole earth? That's a lot of territory to cover and a lot of peoples' hearts to examine. It seems hard to imagine sometimes, that God can be everywhere, know everything, and hear all our prayers at the same time. I mean, how big is God anyway? Can he permeate the whole earth all at once? It takes faith to grasp that, doesn't it?

I think it becomes easier when we remove the humanistic restrictions and features we place on God and just trust that if he has the ability to create the intricacies of the universe that extend billions of light years away, all the way down to DNA, then he's able to accomplish what he says in that verse. The universe is a big place and God is bigger than the universe. Yikes!!!

So, we have to exercise our faith. We need to trust that God is personally looking for us so that he can show himself strong on our behalf.

You know what that promise has attached to it?
A contingency.→ We have to have a heart that's completely given over to God. It's not a half-hearted deal. It's an all-or-nothing deal. In other words, nothing is interfering with our relationship with God. We are completely and devotedly his. If that's you, then God's looking for you in order to personally strengthen *you*.

So, if you want guaranteed strength from God, then make sure your heart is in the right place and then remind God of that promise he made.

God is looking for you so he can look out for you.

Day 141 → 'Let' God help you.

Seems like a no brainer, doesn't it? But you'd be surprised how many people struggle with the '*letting*' part. Either they don't know how to let go of control and let God take over, or they don't know how to open the door to God's help.

It may seem in your own life like the door to his help is locked and you can't find the key. The good news is that God has a whole ring of keys that will unlock the doors to his help, his strength, his comfort, his wisdom...you name it. Those keys are found in his promises.

I'll tell you the master key that opens everything in the kingdom of God – *Believing*.
It's mentioned everywhere in God's Word, and to God, it's very important that we do it.

But, it's the *lack* of *belief* that keeps many of us from receiving God's help. We find it hard to *believe* that he'll come through to do what he says he'll do. I fully understand that feeling. I've been there myself. But, nothing's going to change until we pick up that master key of '*believing*' and use it.

Why do we struggle with believing God anyway? Is it because we're not sure if we can trust him? That's seems like a reasonable explanation at times, after all, most of us have never seen God physically, nor heard his voice audibly.

But that's where faith comes in. Believing what God says leaves doubt behind and blindly steps into the unknown with assuredness. Faith makes the choice to believe God even when it doesn't' make any sense to us to step out of the boat and start walking on water.

So what is faith? Read this verse below:
Hebrews 11:1 → *Faith (believing) is being certain in our heart that the things we hope for will come true. It's being convinced of their reality, even if we don't see them at the moment.*

At times your only available means of movment is a leap of faith.

🌳 Day 142 → Roadblock...Roadblock...Roadblock

There's a verse I need to cover, but I really don't want to. I think it's necessary, though, if we're going to have God's peace in our lives. Here it is:
<u>**Romans 8:6**</u> → *Letting our old sin-bent nature (the flesh) control our life just leads to spiritual deadness and ruin. But <u>letting</u> the Holy Spirit guide our thoughts and actions will lead to genuine life and abundant <u>peace</u>*.

ROADBLOCK: There's one roadblock that can keep us from experiencing the *peace* that God offers. Trust me, I know what it is because it has kept me from having peace more times than I care to share. What's the roadblock? → The <u>*'flesh'*</u>.

What is the 'flesh'? → It's the part of us that functions apart from God's influence. It's the part of us that wants our own way. It's '<u>self</u>'...the root of the phrase '<u>self</u>-centered' ...the root of the word '<u>self</u>ishness'. It's my nickname...at least that's what I've been told at times.

Don't let your '*flesh'* become a roadblock for you.
How do you do that? → By <u>*letting*</u> the Holy Spirit direct your life instead of your 'flesh'.

Some of us might be thinking: *"Well how do you do that?"*
You'd be surprised at how many believers aren't certain how to do it. It starts with acknowledging the Holy Spirit. Jesus said he sent him to live in us so we would have a counselor, a comforter, a friend, and a helper with us at all times. If we just keep the Holy Spirit at a distance, then that's where he'll stay. But he needs to be front and center in our everyday lives. Jesus told us that the Holy Spirit will lead us into all truth. (See John 16:13) And he said in that same verse that the Holy Spirit will speak only what he hears from Jesus.
If we're talking to and listening to the Holy Spirit, he will speak to us in a still small voice. He'll nudge us to guide us in the direction we should go. He'll put in our hearts God's Word to remind us of how to live. That's how we *let* the Holy Spirit guide our lives. But it all comes down to the word – *'Let'*.

<u>**Let God guide you and your destination will be safe.**</u>

Day 143 → <u>We might as well get this straight</u>

God does not intend for his people to live poorly. Some people think that God doesn't want them to have nice things in life. But he does. He wants his people to do well in life. There are many promises about that in the Bible.

Take this verse for example:
Psalm 35:27 → *God takes <u>great delight in the prosperity</u> of his <u>servants</u>.*

You know what? That's <u>a promise</u> and we should look at it that way. God really enjoys it when his people do well in life. Accept that as a fact. That means God really enjoys it when *you* do well in life. <u>And as a side note</u>, it doesn't say anywhere in the Bible that God takes delight in the physical, emotional, or mental suffering of poverty in the lives of his children. He delights in their prosperity. That's what makes him happy. That's what he desires for us. It was built into his original plan for mankind.

But, just as that verse says, God delights in the prosperity <u>of his servants</u>. That tells us something. We need to make sure we truly are his <u>servants</u> (which means - doing what he tells us to do, not necessarily what we want to do).

Many people think that the Bible says money is the <u>root</u> of all evil. But, if they look closer, it says the '*love*' of money is the root of all evil. That's telling us not to love and desire money to the point that we become its *servant*...but instead, to love and desire God to the point that we become his servants (fulfilling his good will for our lives).

How many of us don't get that principle right in our daily living and thus we hinder God from trusting us with prosperity.
If we can live out that principle in the paragraph above; if we can live it out in our lives, then God can trust us with prosperity.

<u>While money can't buy us happiness, it certainly let's us choose our own form of misery.</u>   Groucho Marx

Day 144 → What We Need To Watch Out For:
Our own words

Matthew 12:34 Jesus speaking→ *What we say with our mouths comes from what's filling our hearts.*

Let me ask you this→ What are you telling yourself, or others about your troubles? Does it build your faith up or does it tear it down?

If our heart is full of faith, we'll speak like it. And just the opposite can be true. If our heart is full of doubt, we'll speak like it.

Many of us don't realize that, so we continue to speak words of doubt and unbelief without realizing how it's affecting our faith. We tell our friends and family how big our problems are instead of how big our God is. All that does is weaken our faith.

But remember this: It's not the words that make the difference, it's what's filling our hearts. Is there <u>faith or doubt *behind* our words</u>? The results depend on it...whether to our benefit or our detriment.

Some of us might be thinking, *"Well, what if I feel I don't have enough faith to actually speak words of faith?"*

I get it and I'm with you on that, but remember, it's God's Word that does the work, not the one quoting it.

The power is in his Word, not us. Our *faith* simply activates his Word.
That's why Jesus often said things like, *"Your faith has made you whole"* or *"Your faith has healed you"* or *"Let it be according to your faith"*. It was the person's faith that was the catalyst to activate it.

How about you? Are your words filled with faith or doubt? Make sure that what's filling your heart has its foundation in faith.

Faith believes first. Then faith speaks out what it believes. That's what will lead the heart out of defeat and onward toward victory.

Find your faith and your doubt will starve to death.

Day 145 → You Mean *Whatever* We Ask For?

Take a look at this guarantee:

1 John 3:22 → *We will receive from God whatever we ask for in prayer, because we do exactly what he tells us to do (we obey him) and we do what is pleasing in his sight*.

That word *'because'* is critical here. Don't miss it.
It's like a key that opens a locked door.
It's *because* we're doing *exactly* what he tells us to do that gives us the right to ask what we ask for.

Unfortunately, if we don't do what God tells us to then we might be waiting a long time for our prayers to be answered.

People don't like to hear that. They want to believe that God is going to hear their prayers and answer them no matter what. But God's pretty specific here.

If you want to receive whatever you're asking for from God, then do these 2 things:

1) Do what he tells you to do.
2) Do what's pleasing in his sight.

Some of us might be asking, *"Well, aren't those two things one and the same?"*

Nope. The first refers to what he expressly tells us to do.
The second may not have a command behind it, but we know it's the right thing to do and that it pleases God.
Here's an example of what I mean → Helping a little old lady cross a busy crosswalk. It may not be a command, but we know it's the right thing to do. Yeah, I know…it sounds cliché (helping a little old lady to cross the street. Yikes!) but you get the idea, right?

I think many of us read that verse that's at the top of the page an know what it says…but that's as far as it goes. I think we need to take it seriously, with the full realization that it is a key that unlocks the door to answered prayer. How about you?

God is more eager to answer the prayers of his children than they are to ask. John Macarther

Day 146 → <u>I Need To Make A Point Here.</u>

There are many believers who never really experience God rescuing them out of trouble. Why is that?
It's often because they get tired of waiting for God to act, so they take God's job away from him and start fixing it on their own, only to mess it up more.

Or, instead of walking close beside him day after day, they *wait* until trouble comes their way before they finally call on him for help. That's called throwing God a Hail-Mary pass.
And, because they haven't developed their faith, which comes from walking closely with God in the good times and the bad times, they don't quite know how to use faith when they need it.

So, what do we do about that?
<u>James 4:8</u> **says** → *Draw closer to God and he will draw closer to you.*

Here's the thing→ If we want God to rescue us in the bad times, then we have to get close to him in the good times.
Why? Because God responds to our faith...not just our needs. We have to develop our faith so we're ready to use it when we really need it.
It's our belief and trust in his wisdom and his abilities and his power that moves him to respond, not just because we're in a bad situation.

<u>**And you know what?**</u> We'll never be able to develop the trust and faith we need in tough times if we don't spend the time getting to know him and drawing close to him in the good times.

Now I know I'm preachin' to the choir, so to speak. I know neither you nor I struggle with this. But for those of us who have been struggling to get closer to God, just take that simple verse above as a promise from God. If we really buckle down and take the time to read his written Word, (which is his spoken word in writing) and do what it says; and if we sit and talk to God and then be quiet and listen, he'll talk back to us. That's what drawing close to God is all about. Every day, do something that will lead you closer to God.

<u>If God seems far awa;y...guess who moved?</u>

Day 147 → So, here's a thing I need to bring up

<u>Ephesians 6:11</u> → *Put on all of God's armor so that you'll be able to defend yourself and stand against the wiles, schemes, and tricks of the evil-one.*

Trouble often comes our way because of <u>attacks from the spiritual realm</u>. How often have you found yourself drawing closer to God and "bam!", coming out of left field, you get smacked in the head with trouble you didn't ask for? Why is that?

It's because you're one of God's children and that makes you an enemy of those spiritual entities who hate God.

Why do they hate God? They hate him for casting them out of heaven and dooming them to an eternity of darkness and separation from all things good. So, they lash out at God's children.

I think we all need to remember that we're not just fighting battles in this earthly realm, but we are fighting battles in the spiritual realm as well. These enemies of our souls are no lightweights. They mean business. They aim to rob us of things we hold dear in life. They aim to steal our happiness, our faith, our peace. They even aim to kill us if they can.

That's why the apostle Paul tells us to put on and <u>wear God's spiritual armor</u>, so we can withstand the attacks of these spiritual forces. That's what armor does. It prevents the enemy from harming us.

Can you picture yourself walking around with a helmet and a breastplate and a sword? Me neither, but don't worry, it's invisible. It's God's *spiritual* armor, and that's what we're supposed to wear if we don't want to be spiritually defeated.

Do you have your armor on or did you misplace it? Sometimes I think many of us don't take spiritual warfare as seriously as we should. As a result, many of us are wounded and crippled, on the sidelines instead of the frontlines. How can we be victorious like that?

<u>If you are a Christian and don't know the Word of God, then you are a soldier without a sword.</u>

Day 148 → Surrender...Resist...Flee

If we want to win the battles we go through in life, then we need to make sure we're *surrendered* to God.

Take a look at this guarantee:

James 4:7 → *Surrender yourselves to God. Then, resist (fight) against the evil-one and he will flee from you.*

- The meaning of the word '***surrender***' in the Greek, is *to relinquish control and submit yourself under the authority and rulership of another.* – In our case that would be God.

- The meaning of the word '***resist***' in the Greek, is *to set yourself in contradiction to, to fight against.* – In our case, that would be us against the enemy.

- The meaning of the word '***flee***' in the Greek, is *to vanish, to run away from something abhorrent.* – That would be the enemy fleeing from us, rather than us from them.

When we surrender ourselves to God, we relinquish control over our lives. We surrender to his authority and his rule over us as our king. It also means we stop doing things in our own strength and start using the strength our King offers us.

When God is in control of our lives, he's going to protect us. And, you know what? The enemy has no other option but to flee. Why would the enemy flee? Because now we're under the power and protection of God. No enemy can prevail against God. Before, when we were out from under God's umbrella of protection, we were wide open to the arrows of the enemy. But with Almighty God protecting us, the enemy knows they don't stand a chance. Sometimes I think the enemy fears God more than we do. They won't mess around with the God of the universe. Do we?

God says: *Either you're on my side or you're in my way.*

Day 149 → Who's Hand Are You Holding Anyway!

<u>Isaiah 41:13</u> → *I, the Lord Your God, am the one who <u>holds your right hand</u>, and I say to you, 'Don't be anxious or afraid, I am here to <u>help</u> you.'*

I think when God speaks, we sometimes don't take him very seriously. When God says he's holding our hand, do we believe it? Imagine what it would feel like. Do you remember what when you held someone's hand and It felt safe, strong, and comforting? If God's holding our hand, shouldn't it feel the same way? When he offers his hand to us…we need to take it.

When God says not to worry or be afraid <u>because</u> he's holding our hand and he's here to help us, then we need to take him at his word, and *stop* our worrying and fear. It's simple when you think about it. **You know why God spoke those words**? Because he wanted us to know he's right there with us, and whether it feels like it or not, he's still there holding our hand. We just have to trust what he's saying. Imagine holding God's hand and us insisting on being worried, anxious, and afraid. That wouldn't work, would it?

And don't forget that God is declaring that he's holding your *right* hand. When kings in the Old Testament held up their right hand in battle, it was a sign of victory…that the battle is being won. And here's the thing we need to continually remember.→ God is <u>always</u> victorious…I mean *'always'*. So, guess what? If he's holding up our right hand, we'll be victorious as well. In other words, we won't lose. So, believe it.

Want some <u>help</u> from God? Well, he's holding out his hand. All you have to do is take it. He'll lift it up as sign for all to see that the battle is being won! And what do you suppose the outcome will be for you? – Victory! All we have to do is not let go, right? It may not always feel like a victory, but if you make sure to see it through God's lens, you'll begin to see the *good* in the bad stuff that happens to you. Can there actually be any good in the rotten stuff that happens to us? Well…I'll let you answer that. ☺

<u>*No matter what you face in your life, take God's hand and never let go.*</u>

Day 150 → The Senseless Horse

Take a look at this guarantee:

Psalm 32:8 → *I, God, will guide you* (meaning - make plain and show you the way) *along the paths you should choose* (meaning - the roads you should travel, the decisions you should make, the course of life you should take)…*And, my eye will be upon you, to watch over you* (meaning - to make sure you're safe and staying on the right path). ***But, make sure you don't act like a senseless horse*** *that lacks understanding, that needs a bit in its mouth to keep it under control or else it will not come with you.*

Why would God tell us not to act like a horse that kicks and bucks and resists its owner? Well, that's a key point in that verse above. It's the clincher to that promise:

Have you ever seen those barrel racing horses? They're turning this way and that way, as if they know exactly what the rider wants. All the rider has to do is gently nudge the side of the horse with his heel and the horse will go in the direction its owner wants. It seems effortless, doesn't it?

We need to be like that, so sensitive to God's nudges that we understand when he wants us to turn left or right. There are two things involved with that:

1) sensitivity to God's nudges.
2) Cooperating with the one who's nudging.

I think we need to do a heart-check every few days, if not every day. Are we being sensitive to the nudges of God? And when we do feel his nudge, do we make the decision to cooperate with him so he can take us where he wants us to go? If you think about it, that's what guidance from God is all about, isn't it?

God does not guide those who want to run their own life.

Thank you for reading this <u>Devotional</u>.

If you haven't read my book **God's Guarantees**, I would love for you to check it out. This Devotional was based on that book.

You can find **God's Guarantees** by Geoffrey Kilgore on <u>Amazon</u>.

Also, I would also love to hear from you. You can reach out to me via email at:

gkwalkingthewalk@gmail.com

====================

Hey, if you enjoyed this Devotional, I would be honored to receive a short <u>review</u> on Amazon, which consists of simply saying whether or not you liked the book and whether you would recommend it to others. That's it. That's a review. Reviews encourage others to check out the book.
Many people don't know where to go on Amazon to do it, let alone how to do it. It's actually pretty easy. <u>The steps are on the next page</u>.

How To Leave A Review Of This Book On Amazon

2 Basic Rules:
1) The book does not have to be purchased on Amazon to leave a review.
2) You must have an active Amazon account.

✦ If you purchased this book on Amazon
7 Super Easy Steps

1) Go to **your account page** and click on **Orders**.
2) **Find the book on the order page** and click the box on the right that says **Write A Product Review**.
3) Give a **star rating** (5 stars being the best)
4) (This step is *optional*) Leaving a photo of the book, but this is **not required**.
5) In the **Add A Headline** box → Give a simple title for your review.
6) In the **Add A Review** box → **Remember** it can just be a short paragraph or as long as you want to make it.
To help you out, here are 3 questions to answer →
Put them together and you've got a book review. ☺
1) Did you like the book?
2) Is there one particular part of the book you liked?
3) Would you recommend it to a friend?
7) Finally....**DON'T FORGET** to click the **Submit** button

---

If you *didn't* buy the book on Amazon, see next page.

✦ If you did *not* purchase the book on Amazon
7 Super Easy Steps

1) Look up the **book title** on Amazon → <u>God's Guarantees</u> by Geoffrey Kilgore
2) On the book page….**scroll all the way down** until you see (<u>on the left-hand side</u>) - **Customer Reviews** with the breakdown of the star ratings. → Just below the stars you will see **Review This Product**. Click on the box that says **Write A Customer Review**.
3) Give a **<u>star rating</u>** (5 stars being the best)
4)) (This step is *optional*) Leaving a photo of the book, but this is **not required**.
5) In the **<u>Add A Headline</u>** box → Give a simple title for you review
6) In the **<u>Add A Review</u>** box → **Remember** it can just be a short paragraph or as long as you want to make it.

To help you out, here are 3 questions to answer →
Put them together and you've got a book review. ☺
1) Did you like the book?
2) Is there one particular part of the book you   liked?
3) Would you recommend it to a friend?

7) Finally….**DON'T FORGET** to click the **<u>Submit</u>** button